Vegetables on the Grill

A Garden-Grilling Cookbook

Plus–Recipes for Meats, Seafoods, Pastas & Side Dishes!

by Shifra Stein

Pig Out Publications, Inc.

Copyright © 1998 by Shifra Stein
Editor: Dee Barwick
Cover and Text Design: Premila Malik Borchardt
Cover Photo: © David Morris/MIDWE**STOCK**
Printed in the United States of America
ISBN: 0-925175-30-7

Pig Out Publications, Inc.
4245 Walnut Street, Kansas City, Missouri 64111

Pig Out Publications, Inc., specializes in publishing and distributing barbecue and grilling cookbooks and equipment. Authors are available for speaking engagements. To book authors and/or place orders, contact our marketing department at (816)531-3119 or e-mail us at kadler@unicom.net.

ACKNOWLEDGMENTS

My heartfelt thanks to all the red wigglers who made this book possible. Much appreciation, too, to my asparagus, beets, broccoli, Brussels sprouts, carrots, cauliflower, corn, eggplant, fennel, garlic, shallots, green beans, greens, leeks, onions, and scallions, peas, peppers, potatoes, tomatoes, zucchini and other squash who have shared their secrets with me year after year.

I am grateful also to my dill for bringing me black swallowtails, to my lemon verbena, for its aroma, and to all my other herbs for their magnificent taste and flavor.

I would also like to thank Bob whose invaluable help as digger and planter made my garden possible. My appreciation also to Moke whose love of nature has brought me joy, and to my Mother, who let me walk through her garden when I was a child.

Oh, and I also want to thank my dog, Mickey, for not peeing on the broccoli last year.

To own a bit of ground, to scratch it with a hoe, to plant seeds, and watch the renewal of life—this is the commonest delight of the race, the most satisfactory thing one can do.
Charles Dudley Warner

CONTENTS

PREFACE

This book offers a winning combination of America's two best-loved pas-times—outdoor cooking and gardening. The essays are written for gardeners, as well as those who appreciate the taste of fresh produce from a local farm stand or gourmet grocer.

The earthy flavors of smoky corn, fresh spring onions, and flavorful herbs are celebrated in an abundance of essays and recipes that offer help for fami-lies who live in a hectic world. The focus is on taste and nutrition, with "fast food" grilling techniques offered as an alternative to the tired cholesterol-laden burgers, fries, and microwaved dinners.

This is real food for people who need to take a little time to slow down and smell the mint. The quick and easy recipes included here can make life a little easier (and a little healthier).

Within these pages are the benefits reaped from both garden and grill: the use of fresh produce along with the beauty and abundance of growing things, are alternatives to a stressed-out world of canned, frozen, tasteless, television nights.

INTRODUCTION
Gardening from the Ground Up

I was once gardening-challenged. I bought my vegetables at the store, and worse, I bought frozen. I was doomed as doomed could be. One day, when I finally shut down my laptop long enough to look out my window, I found sunshine in my back yard, and good dirt, too.

I picked up a number of excellent gardening books and started reading. I studied the labels on the seed packets for the best directions. I gathered courage, girded my pork loins, and set seeds and seedlings in the ground. Alas, I was struck by the curse of the black thumb. I killed everything I planted, except weeds—I grew glorious weeds.

One day a market vendor saw me poking around at his tomatoes. He was going to close up for the day and gave me a great buy on 17 badly wilted and scraggly tomato plants. I thought they were "Kentucky Wonders," so I bought them. Despite my ignorance, I managed to grow many well-formed, highly tasty tomatoes. This emboldened me enough to take the next step: tilling the soil. I unearthed in the process some old bones and coins left by former residents. In their place, I planted all manner of things including squash and strawberries which quickly took over the entire garden. I cut back on plants that sprawled, and concentrated on those that gave me more taste for less space.

This book is the result of some years of experimentation in growing and grilling garden vegetables. I don't presume to be a gourmet cook, nor am I an expert master gardener. I am just a busy person who likes to eat well and knows from experience what to plant and how to plant it. I plant the best-tasting vegetables that offer the most vitamins and minerals for the least amount of time and money invested.

I don't use pesticides, or other noxious things that can kill weeds, along with other living things. If I get weeds, I yank them out. A little weed-pulling can cut down your counseling bills considerably. Also, poking around in dirt can do wonders for your sanity.

Like other sane gardeners, I talk to my plants, urging them on and thanking them for being nice enough to provide me with a bountiful crop at harvest time. I do this because I believe that all growing things do better when they are cared for. There are skeptics who think plants feel nothing at all, but this defies logic. It is more rational to assume that whatever made this earth and the things in it, made them to correspond with its own nature. Therefore, it is fair to assume that humans and tomatoes have some things in common. Plants, like kids, will grow to maturity with or without tender loving care, but they thrive and flourish when they are loved.

Every year I have a garden filled with great, gorgeous vegetables. I plant nothing fancy, nor difficult to grow. Each summer, I gain more knowledge about plants, dirt, earthworms, and compost. But mostly I'm learning about how to enjoy myself and I wanted to share some of what I've learned with you. Also, I wanted to let you know that if I can do this stuff, so can you.

GARDENING BASICS
Tips, Tools, and Techniques

If you haven't gardened before, buy a book that has simple "how-to" advice and nice pictures. Gardening publications by Sunset Books and Ortho books are excellent beginner's guides. One of the best garden manuals on the market is *The Cook's Garden,* by Shepherd and Ellen Ogden, two very knowledgeable people who are much better gardeners than I am. They do it for a living; I don't. I just like fooling around with dirt and playing with eggplant.

Gardners plant according to the average dates of the last killing frost in spring and the first killing frost in fall. Many gardening books provide charts that provide information about when to expect these cold snaps in your area. For example, in Napa, California the last spring frost is expected in mid-January and the first fall frost around mid-December. In Kansas City, Missouri we expect our last spring frost in mid-April, followed by a first fall frost around mid-October.

On the back of most seed packets you'll find information on planting time according to what zone you live in. I live in Missouri, so my planting season may be different from your own. For example, on the back of my packet of cucumber seeds, the zones are clearly marked. In Florida (Zone 1), cucumbers can be planted September through February; in Georgia (Zone 2), late March through June; in Missouri (Zone 3), late April through June; in North Dakota (Zone 4), late May or June.

Since I live in Missouri, the gardening tips and planting times I've given in this book may not coincide exactly with your area. To apply the information to fit your needs, simply adapt it for the region in which you live.

Once you know your zone, begin with a basic garden plan, arranging plants according to type and height, and group annuals and perennials together. Learn what crops need to be planted in early spring, summer, and early fall and how the differences between cold sensitive and cold resistant plants can affect the success of your garden. After this, read up on preventing weeds, killing weeds, weeding the lawn, and weeding the garden. If you're still hanging in there—you've passed the first test. You can then move on to insect problems, feeding, watering, pruning, disease prevention, soil management, composting, and other fun-filled activities.

When you start to garden, you'll make mistakes, but so what? You'll learn from them.

As anxious as you may be to get started, wait until you've boned up on information about how the physical makeup of your soil will affect plant growth. This way there won't be surprises. If you learn that you have compact soil, you'll find that this stunts roots and produces spindly crops. Coarse soil allows moisture to drain too rapidly, keeping plants continually thirsty. Armed with information, you can then add the right nutrients to it like manure, compost, and other organic fertilizers to keep it "friable," or workable. I also add earthworms because they are so cute and because they aerate the soil.

Nitrogen makes healthy green leaves, phosphorous creates good root systems, and potassium builds disease resistance. Some plants, like tomatoes and peppers, need more phosphorous. Some—like lettuce—need more nitrogen. Root crops such as carrots crave potassium.

Chemical fertilizers contain the three basic elements needed for plant growth. You can control the amount of nutrients by reading the label. A label shows you the ratio of nitrogen, phosphorus, and potassium to each other. For example, a fertilizer high in nitrogen will have a formula of 10-6-4, meaning that it contains 10 percent nitrogen, six percent phosphorus, and 4 percent potassium. If root crops are grown, you need a fertilizer low in nitrogen, but equal in phosphorous and potassium (5-10-10). Manufacturers use the letters N,P,K for nitrogen, phosphorus, and potassium, always in that order.

Common natural sources for nitrogen are blood meal, cottonseed meal, and fish emulsion or scraps. Phosphorus sources include phosphate rock, fish scraps, and cottonseed meal. Natural sources for potassium include wood ashes, seawood, and tobacco stems. Although bone meal is also an excellent source for nitrogen and phosphorus, I am waiting until I read that there is conclusive evidence showing no health-related problems as a result of using it.

Your soil pH is another factor that can influence healthy plant growth. The technical term, pH, refers to acidity or alkalinity. If nothing is growing where you've planted it, and you've added all the fertilizer in the world, and watered it patiently—the problem may stem from the wrong soil pH. Adding lime for alkalinity or sulfur to acidify the soil can help when nothing else does. Your local garden center should have soil testing kits and you can send core samples to your State Agricultural Experiment Station. However, you can tell whether a soil is acid or alkaline by simply watching to see what grows and what doesn't. Two vegetables, beets and potatoes, can quickly give you an indication of what kind of soil you have. Beets do poorly in acid conditions while potatoes positively thrive in it. So, logic dictates that if you have acid soil, and want to grow beets, you would add some alkaline "sweetener" to your garden. Add some sulfur to alkaline soil to grow potatoes.

When you've learned all you can about soil pH, and the four stages of seed-growing (from starting them indoors in flats, to setting them out in the garden), you will have acquired enough knowledge to manage your garden quite well.

There are a few garden gadgets you'll need to get started. These include a spading fork for turning and breaking up the soil, a hoe for weeding, a watering can, garden hose or garden sprinkler-soaker system, a rake, some twine, wire cages for supporting tomatoes, and wooden stakes for destroying vampires and propping up plants that need something to lean on. There are so many vegetable varieties available that, for a busy person, it may be more expedient to use seedlings, rather than go through the process of seed germination, transplanting, and hardening off which is quite time-consuming. However, if you grow from seed, there are more varieties of plants from which to choose and buying seed is a much more cost-effective way to plant if you have a lot of room and a lot of hungry mouths to feed.

Seedlings, on the other hand, can be planted more easily. Just stick them in the proper soil when the time is right, protect them from pests, water them, and you should have great success.

Growing vegetables isn't difficult. It doesn't take magic; but it does take persistence. I will share with you six rules that work for me.

Stein's Stupidly Simple Rules For Success

❦

Have plenty of good dirt, organic fertilizer, water,
and sun available for your plants.

❦

Use disease resistant varieties for better yields.

❦

Read the seed packet directions, or get directions
for planting from your gardening center.

❦

If your plants can't tolerate cool weather,
don't plant them in cool weather.

❦

If your plants can't tolerate hot weather,
don't plant them in hot weather.

❦

If you can't tolerate sun, dirt, bugs, worms,
or manure—don't garden.

GRILLING BASICS
Tips, Tools, and Techniques

GRILLING

When you grill, you cook over a direct heat source. Fuel sources can be gas, electric, and charcoal/hardwood. Gas and electric grills make life easier, since they're quick starting and easy to clean. Just follow the manufacturer's directions for success. Charcoal grills come in all sizes and shapes, with or without covers. The kettle-shaped grill is the most popular for home use and also very economical.

STARTING THE FIRE

Gas grills are simple to start. All you do is turn them on and light 'em up. There's no muss, no fuss, and no waiting. Charcoal fires can be started several ecologically safe ways. Mound the charcoal onto the lower fire grate of the grill, except when using a charcoal chimney. When the coals are hot, spread them out in an even layer on the fire grate. This is the direct cooking area. Use the following items for easy fire-starting:

The charcoal chimney is a straight upright cylindrical metal cannister. Fill the chimney with 15-20 briquettes. Place it on a nonflammable surface, such as concrete, or the grill top, and put crumpled paper in the bottom. Light the paper and let the coals get hot (it takes about 15 minutes). Empty the hot coals onto the lower fire rack of the grill.

The electric starter is an easy way to start a fire. You'll probably need an outdoor electrical outlet or extension cord. Place the coil on the lower rack of the grill and stack charcoal on top of it. Plug it in and the fire will start in about 10 minutes. Remove the coil and let the starter cool on a nonflammable surface, out of the reach of children and pets.

Solid starters are compressed wood blocks or sticks treated with flammable substances such as paraffin. They are easy to ignite and don't give off a chemical odor. Two or three will easily light the charcoal. Simply set them on top of or beside the briquettes and ignite.

Do not use lighter fluids. They can cause flare-ups. Avoid using paper as kindling, and always have plenty of water or baking soda within reach to suppress overzealous flames.

GRILLING TIME AND TEMPERATURE

Grill directly over hot to medium-hot fires, depending on the distance your grill rack sits from the fire. In gas grills, the fire is ready instantaneously and, just like any other oven, you have heat controls you can turn up or down, for a hotter or lower flame.

In charcoal grills the fire is ready when the flame subsides and the coals are glowing red and beginning to ash over. You can recognize a medium-hot fire when the coals are no longer red, but ashen. Another test to gauge the temperature is to hold your hand five inches above the heat source. Make sure that the grill rack is clean of grease before you do this little trick, or you could light up your hand instead. If you can only hold your hand there for about two seconds, you're fire is hot; three to four seconds is a medium hot fire, and five to six seconds is a low fire. Never allow a child to test the grill for you.

Estimating cooking times can be a challenge. This is because the time required to cook vegetables or meat varies due to the kind of grill used, heat of the fire, type of coals used, and the distance the heat source is from the grill rack. Use the suggested cooking times given in each recipe. Some people rely on meat thermometers to ensure that the food is cooked to the recommended safe internal temperatures.

UTENSILS FOR VEGETABLE GRILLING

Several basic tools make grilling vegetables a cinch. A barbecue and grill shop or a mail order supply house usually keeps professional utensils that are superior in quality and durability. Long handles are preferable on everything to keep you a safe distance from the fire.

You will need:

A wire brush. The stiffer, the better. It should have a metal scraper on one end to make cleaning the grill a simple job (tackle this while the grill is still warm).

A basting brush. One with natural bristles is best for brushing oil on the grill before you start the fire to prevent sticking. Get a separate brush for basting foods during cooking.

Heat resistant mitts. These offer the best hand protection, especially when you need to touch any hot metals during the grilling process.

Spray bottle. Keep this filled with water by the grill to douse flare-ups. A garden hose within quick reaching distance can substitute, but make sure the water is turned on!

Spatula. A long, wooden-handled offset spatula with a five to six inch blade is helpful for turning items vegetables, burgers, and fish filets. Grease it well to avoid sticking.

Tongs. Long-handled, spring-loaded tongs are easier to use than the scissor type. They are great for turning vegetables, chicken, steaks, skewers, and the like.

Grill racks. These are grates placed on top of the grill to accommodate small or delicate items such as vegetables, fish fillets, scallops, and shrimp. Always grease the grill rack before using so food won't stick.

Hinged grill baskets. These hold food in place and make turning an easy process. Grease the baskets before using.

Grill woks. The grill wok makes "stir-grilling" possible. The wok has perforated holes to let in the smoky flavor and sits directly on top of the grill. Stir-grill vegetables and tender meats by tossing with wooden paddles. The grill wok enables totally oil-free cooking and is a staple with health-conscious cooks.

Herb grill rack. Another way to use your herbs is by searing their flavor into your meat, fish, or vegetables. The herb grill rack allows you to place the herbs in between the two mesh pieces, then secure the hinge shut. You can place your favorite vegetables or meat over the herb grill rack, and cook. Although the herb grill racks tout easy clean-up, in most cases I've found it necessary to scrub hard at the blackened remains of herbs fused like glue to the supposedly non-stick metal surfaces. So use non-stick spray on both sides of the rack for easy clean-up.

Skewers. Either wood or metal skewers can be used to thread vegetables and meat loosely together prior to placing them on the grill to cook. Wooden or bamboo skewers should be soaked for at least 30 minutes before using so the ends won't char during grilling. Flat metal skewers or double skewers are preferred, so that cubed food doesn't spin while turning.

FLAVOR ENHANCERS

Vegetables, fish, and seafood pick up marinade flavors quickly. Marinating for 15 minutes to an hour should be sufficient. Tougher cuts of meat may marinate several hours or overnight in the refrigerator.

Woods and herbs added to the grill fire offer another way to get more taste. Some vegetables cook so quickly over a hot fire that the addition of soaked wood chips or herbs will not penetrate effectively. If you want more smoke flavor while you're grilling, use a medium fire, and close the lid for a few minutes for best results.

Wood chips are best for quick cooking. Some people soak their chips for about 30 minutes prior to grilling or keep a plastic container filled with wood chips in water, then throw a handful on the fire.

While this works well for charcoal grilling, don't try it with gas grilling. Loose wood chips can gum up the heating elements in a gas grill. To avoid this, wrap soaked wood chips in aluminum foil, poke some holes in the foil to let out the smoke, and place the foil over the heat source. Or you may use a small metal wood chip box available at grill centers.

Choose hardwoods that burn hot, like mesquite. You can also use hickory, cherry, oak, alder, pear, peach, and apple wood or grapevines.

Dried herbs or fresh herbs can also be used to flavor your vegetables and meats. You can use an herb grill rack for fresh herbs or toss some dry herbs onto your charcoal fire for an aromatic experience.

Personally, I do something even simpler. If I want to add an herb flavor to my grilling, I just pick a bunch of basil, tarragon, oregano, or whatever from my garden, and place it on top of my vegetables or meat to cook. The herb flavor permeates the food from the top down and gives it a wonderful taste.

For gas grills, it's best to use an herb grill rack or wrap your dried herbs in foil that has holes punched in it. Again this is more an aromatic experience for the grillers than it is for the food, but it's fun.

HERBS

No garden would be complete without herbs. A summer without a snip of fresh basil is like a winter without light. Herbs complete a recipe, adding character, flavor, and excitement. Every summer I look forward to the smell and feel of fresh herbs that I use for grilling, salad-making, vinegars, and other culinary uses.

If I am not following a particular recipe, but wish to add an herb flavor to my dish, I just choose something tasty from from my garden: basil, or tarragon, or perhaps a sprig of rosemary. I then place it on top of the vegetable or meat, letting the flavor permeate the food while the herb's aroma fills my back yard with a heady fragrance.

Growing herbs is easier than making peanut butter and jelly sandwiches. All you need is sunny, well-drained soil that is loamy, or you can grow herbs in containers and raised beds. Herbs like an alkaline pH, so add some dolomite or eggshells in the fall before planting along with plenty of organic matter. With an abundance of sunshine and warm weather, your herbs should flourish.

Some garden herbs and vegetables do affect the health of their garden companions and there are a few which supposedly repel pests. Cabbage moths seem to lay fewer eggs on cabbages sprayed with thyme or sage extract. Although all the evidence isn't in, some studies have found that nasturtiums seem to repel Colorado potato beetles and aphids. Radishes have been touted as "traps" for cabbage maggots, and borage presumably keeps Japanese beetles away from other precious plants.

Herbs can also attract beneficial bugs. Thyme, rosemary, and mint lure creeping predators like spiders. Dill, anise and carrots host parasitic wasps that feed on mealybugs and aphids. You may not like wasps, or bees, either, but they help pollinate the garden and without these creatures, it would be impossible for plants to bear fruit.

Used for their fragrance as well as their substance, herbs produce aromatic scents that are unique. Lemon verbena, lemon balm, and peppermint can wake up the senses. Borage, or cinnamon basil, rubbed between the fingers, can soothe the nerves and quiet the mind. You can cut bouquets of fresh herbs and keep them in your kitchen so they are handy to snip during cooking.

A potpourri of dried, aromatic herbs can be used outside the kitchen, too. Basil, bay, cardamom seeds, cinnamon, cloves, coriander seeds, lemon verbena, marjoram, mint, rosemary, sage, thyme, scented geraniums and flowers can be made into herb bouquets and set in bowls around the house to add a lovely aroma to your rooms.

One of my favorite herbs is dill, which I also use in my butterfly garden. Dill is graceful and delicate and its foliage can be used in salads, and its seeds in soups. It is also the host plant for the black swallowtail butterfly. So if you see little chartreuse and black caterpillars climbing all over your dill, do not pluck them off and destroy them. Instead, think about sharing your dill with these creatures who are actually butterflies in drag.

I am crazy about black swallowtails and I admit that I go to great lengths to obtain the caterpillars. I even scrounge around at garage sales, hoping to find an unsold pot of dill, preferably with caterpillars affixed to it. Last year at a sale I found three swallowtail caterpillars busily eating their weight in dill.

The owner, who could care less about the "bugs" as she called them, gave me a ridiculous price on her scraggly dill. I declined the buy, asking instead if I could have the caterpillars. She seemed shocked, but then a suspicious gleam crept into her eyes as she totalled up the value of the tiny creatures in her head. She told me I could have just one—but only if I bought something. So I gave her 25 cents for a used smelly sponge and took home a plump, fuzzy fellow that I immediately placed on my own dill. I even fenced the dill so no-one would harm it. To my dismay, the caterpillar disappeared a couple of days later. I was devastated. Something had eaten it after all. Imagine my surprise when, one morning, I saw a black swallowtail flitting over the dill, on his way out of town. So I guess the lousy sponge was worth it, after all.

Fines herbes are a classic herb mix of French haute cuisine. They include equal parts chervil, chives, parsley, and tarragon. Other mild herbs may be substituted or added:

Chervil. This looks like parsley and tastes like mild anise. I use chervil, as well as parsley, depending on my mood.

Chives. With their onion-like flavor, chives grow wild all over my neighborhood. You can start them by taking a clump from an already established plant and sticking it in the ground. I use the lovely purple flowers too, to garnish my salads.

Marjoram. Many people like the flavor of this herb, calling it "delicate." Maybe so, but I've never found the taste of marjoram particularly thrilling. You can use it in salad or casseroles, and to flavor meat. Personally I prefer oregano, but, then, I have hearty tastes.

Parsley. Easy to start from seed in containers, it may be transplanted in summer, or sown directly in soil. I mix flat-leafed Italian parsley in with my curly varieties and have plenty of seasoning for soups, salads, and grilling.

Thyme. Used in classic French cooking, thyme can be easily grown, provided you keep the weeds away from it. I use lemon thyme because of the citrus flavor it imparts to my favorite foods, but you can also grow other varieties.

Tarragon. I love tarragon's buttery taste. I use it for eggs, salads, fish, and meats. It's a little more delicate than other herbs and so if you buy seedlings, make sure they're big and hearty, with no root rot or mildew.

Other herbs that are fun to grow are:

Basil varieties include everything from cinnamon, lemon, and licorice, to opal, lemon, and sweet basil. Although many gardeners go to great lengths to grow basil, I do it the easy way. I set out seedlings early when the weather is cool. Later as the ground warms up I sow seed directly. I use sweet basil for cooking and for making pesto.

Coriander, also known as cilantro, is used in Mexican and Asian cooking. The leaves should be picked as the plants mature since coriander quickly goes to seed in hot weather.

Dill, like most herbs, can be sown from seed as soon as the ground warms up. Herbs like good soil. For the purposes of this book, I'm going to cover some of the most popular culinary herbs that are easy to grow and can be used for more than a garnish.

Edible flowers are fun to eat and fun to cultivate. You can really awe your family and friends with flower-topped salads. I *love* the cucumber-flavored taste of velvety leaves and purple flowers of borage so much that I make a special place in my garden for this herb. I also enjoy the peppery flavor of nasturtium leaves and the yellow, orange, and red flowers that make a beautiful salad garnish. The flower ends of chives also make a pungent addition to salads—but you really have to like the taste of onions to use them.

Fennel, like dill, has foliage that works well for salads. All parts of fennel are edible, including the bulb which adds a nice licorice taste to soups and stews.

Lemon Verbena is a plant that more people need to cultivate. I could spend all day rubbing it between my fingers, and inhaling the fragrant aroma. Lemon verbena can be used to flavor tea, and enhance the taste of fish, meat, salads, and vegetables.

Oregano can be planted from seed and, as a perennial will come back from year to year if the soil conditions are right. Greek oregano is especially good for cooking because it imparts a more vigorous flavor than do other varieties.

Rosemary is more fragile than some herbs, rosemary can be purchased already started in containers. Look for plants that are big and healthy to put in the ground. I use rosemary to flavor potatoes, lamb, and other dishes.

Sage is easy to raise, but takes up a lot of room. I use it to season poultry and pork, and to add flavor to sauces. After harvesting, it can be hung up to dry for herbal wreaths and other uses.

ASPARAGUS

A tender harvest of asparagus, fresh with early morning dew, can renew your spirits and dazzle your taste buds. This bright green perennial needs a lot of space, so you need to find a permanent location for it because, if everything works out, you're going to have asparagus for a while.

It takes three years to produce asparagus shoots, so patience is important. The wait is worth it, for their arrival in spring heralds a magical experience that is a cook's delight. Picked fresh the same day you plan to eat it, homegrown asparagus tastes like nothing else.

This interesting vegetable undergoes various incarnations during its lifetime as seeds turn into rhizomes with scraggly roots that you can plant early spring. You can mail-order the rhizomes from garden centers and place them in foot-deep and two-foot-wide trenches, adding manure or compost to ensure growth. The first year when the spears shoot up and produce feathery foliage, don't jump the gun and start picking. The greenery is needed to direct every bit of energy toward the development of a strong root system. Resist the temptation to pick more than a few spears the next year, and by the third year you'll have enough asparagus for several meals.

Purists usually snap off the spears at the breaking point, but you can enjoy the stalk as well since homegrown asparagus is more tender and tasty than store-bought.

Some people I know freeze asparagus, blanching the stalks in boiling water for a couple of minutes, and placing the spears in plastic bags prior to freezing. However, my motto is: plant it; pick it; and eat it because if you wait, the flavor won't be the same. Also, in the meantime, while the asparagus sits in the freezer waiting to be eaten, you could get hit by a bus. So what's the point?

The only concern you might have about growing asparagus is that it takes up a lot of space that might otherwise be used to grow another vegetable. So, if you decide to take the time to cultivate it, be someone who truly savors the crop.

Grilled "Roasted" Asparagus

2 pounds asparagus
2 tablespoons extra virgin olive oil
2 tablespoons fresh lime juice
1/2 cup chopped fresh tarragon
1/4 cup chopped fresh dill
Freshly ground pepper

Place asparagus on greased grill rack, and sprinkle with olive oil, lime juice, herbs, and pepper. Grill asparagus over a medium fire for about 10 to 15 minutes, or until crisp tender and slightly charred. Serves 4 to 6.

Citrus-Grilled Asparagus

20-25 firm slender to medium stalks of asparagus, cut diagonally
   into one-inch pieces
8 scallions, sliced diagonally in half-inch pieces

Citrus Marinade
3/4 cup orange juice
1 tablespoon lemon juice
2 teaspoons toasted sesame oil
2 teaspoons teriyaki sauce
1 teaspoon freshly grated ginger

Combine marinade ingredients. Place asparagus and scallions in marinade and let sit in a glass dish for one hour, turning stalks and scallions occasionally. Grease a grill wok or rack and grill asparagus for about 10 to 15 minutes, or until crisp tender and slightly charred. Drizzle remaining marinade over hot asparagus. Serves 4.

Buckwheat Noodles in Sesame-Orange Sauce

1 pound buckwheat noodles or whole wheat noodles, cooked,
    drained and cooled to room temperature
4 teaspoons toasted sesame seeds

Sesame-Orange Sauce

1/4 cup soy sauce (or low-salt Shoyu soy sauce, available at
    health food stores)
1/4 cup teriyaki sauce
1/2 cup toasted sesame oil
1 teaspoon honey
1 teaspoon granulated sugar
1 clove garlic, minced
2 tablespoons fresh orange juice
1 teaspoon freshly grated ginger

Combine soy sauce, teriyaki sauce, toasted sesame oil, honey, sugar, garlic,
orange juice, and ginger in a blender. Toss with noodles in a large bowl.
Sprinkle with sesame seeds. Serves 4.

ℰ∂

You can also toss the noodles with Citrus Grilled Asparagus *for
a tasty variation.*

Grilled Salmon with Rosemary

1-1/2 pounds boneless salmon fillets, skin intact

Marinade
1/4 cup olive oil
2 sprigs fresh rosemary
1/4 cup dry white wine
1 tablespoon fresh lemon juice
1 clove garlic, minced
Salt and freshly ground pepper to taste

Combine marinade ingredients and pour over salmon in a shallow glass dish. Marinate in refrigerator for 30 minutes. Remove salmon for grilling. Pour marinade into a saucepan and bring to a boil. Boil for 1 minute, remove from heat and set aside. Place salmon on a grill topper, flesh-side down. Grill over hot coals for about five minutes, then turn over and continue grilling for five minutes more. Spoon cooked marinade over fillets and serve. Serves 4.

Grilled Salmon Steaks with Dill and Caper Butter

4 (8 ounce) salmon steaks
Dill and Caper Butter

Brush salmon with softened *Dill and Caper Butter*. Grill over hot coals for 5 minutes per side, basting continuously until fish is brown on the outside and cooked well on the inside. Serves 4.

Dill and Caper Butter
1 stick butter, softened
1/2 bunch dill, finely chopped
3 tablespoons capers, drained and crushed
1 teaspoon lemon zest

Combine butter with dill, capers and zest. Place in middle of foil or plastic wrap and roll into a cylinder. Wrap and chill or freeze until ready to use.

BEETS

To beet or not to beet, that is the question. Whether 'tis nobler to make borscht, than to buy it, is your choice. For years the lowly beet has been served up in various incarnations: steamed, creamed, served fresh in salads; and made into borscht. Yet I believe that nothing compares to beets *grilled,* for the flavor is entirely different.

If you've tried store bought and found them to be somewhat leathery and tasteless, try growing your own. Fresh beets are sweet, crisp and sensational when grilled. You can eat them alone or in tandem with other vegetables such as new potatoes, or swiss chard or with a variety of meats.

Depending on the beets you buy, you can sow seeds in early spring and every three weeks thereafter until the first frost arrives. Plant your beets in well-drained, loamy soil and be sure to leave plenty of room for the beet seeds to grow and prosper. It's a wise practice to thin the rows since you'll get about eight offspring from each seed you plant—or up to nine mature plants from only one seed!

Beets are sensitive to acid soil, so you need to alkalize the soil with something such as wood ash. Add organic matter such as humus and manure to your garden plot well ahead of planting time, so nutrients can be slowly released into the soil. Beets also need water, especially during hot spells when the beet greens tend to wilt. The leaves, themselves, are a delicacy served lightly steamed with lemon butter.

Beet skins are thin and can easily be punctured by a madcap fling with a trowel or other sharp garden tool. Better to pull them up by hand. Baby beet varieties should be picked as soon as they reach the size of golf balls. It's important to dig up these small fry early since they will become more woody the older and bigger they get. Other beets, such as white and golden varieties can grow just short of baseball size and still be tender at picking time.

Grilled Baby Beets
with Scallions and Lemon-Herb Butter

12 baby beets, about 1 inch in diameter, scrubbed and
    trimmed, leaving 2 inches of greens
8 scallions trimmed
Lemon-Herb Butter
Salt and pepper to taste

Parboil the beets for 10 to 15 minutes, or until tender enough to pierce with a fork. Drain, rinse in cold water and pat dry. Heat *Lemon-Herb Butter* in saucepan until melted. When beets have cooled place together with scallions on a grill rack. Brush beets and scallions with butter mixture and sprinkle with salt and pepper. Grill over a hot fire, basting with butter mixture entire time. Grill scallions 4 minutes per side. Grill beets about 4 to 6 minutes per side, or until brown and crunchy on the outside and soft on the inside. Serve remaining butter on the side for dipping. Serves 4.

Lemon-Herb Butter
1 stick (4 ounces) unsalted butter, softened
2 teaspoons fresh lemon juice
2 tablespoons chopped fresh herbs (such as dill, oregano,
    thyme or parsley)
2 garlic cloves, minced (optional)

Combine butter with remaining ingredients. Place butter in middle of sheet of foil or plastic wrap and roll into a cylinder. Wrap and chill or freeze until ready to use.

ℰℐ

*If fresh herbs are not available, substitute 1 teaspoon dried for
1 tablespoon fresh.*

BROCCOLI

Despite the fact that broccoli was never a favorite of President George Bush, I happen to like it and so do millions of other people. It belongs to the cabbage family and is related to the cauliflower, but broccoli outshines its kith and kin in terms of popularity. This is partly because it tastes terrific, and also because it is reputed to boost health and ward off cancer.

So versatile is this veggie that it can be eaten raw, steamed, creamed, grilled, and chilled, not to mention marinated, pureed, and stir-fried. Broccoli is also simple to grow as long as you use broccoli logic. If you start with seedlings, avoid those that have thick stems and yellowed or discolored leaves. Feed your broccoli manure that's well worked into the soil and cultivate your plants immediately before the weeds get in the way. Even after you pick the largest head, other buds will appear, so don't rip broccoli out of the ground before you eat all there is to eat.

The exciting part begins when the broccoli heads get really big. Every year the race is on between me and the finches to see who can get to the pickins' first. The birds are so broccoli-crazed, I have to cover my plants with a net to keep them out. Even so, it is a futile effort. Last year I planted a crop for the birds, and a separate crop for me. I even put up a sign that said "Birds Keep Out" to discourage them from nibbling away at my patch. Either they were far too clever, or they couldn't read the message, for they continued in their relentless pursuit of my plants. I finally resigned myself to snatching up what I could before they snarfed it all down.

Fortunately broccoli just keeps going all summer long, like the "Energizer Bunny." So both the birds and I usually get our fair share. The time to clip the head is before the florets open and you can see the yellow inside. I cut the broccoli stem about four inches below the head and leave the stalk so it can produce new shoots. Cutting the sprouting heads just seems to stimulate the broccoli to produce more and more shoots making the growing of this plant a perfect choice for the gardening-impaired.

Parmesan-Grilled Broccoli

1 large bunch broccoli, preferably garden-fresh
1/2 cup freshly grated Parmesan cheese
3 tablespoons extra-virgin olive oil
2 large garlic cloves, minced
5 fresh basil leaves, torn in pieces

Trim broccoli stalks, remove leaves and peel stalks with a vegetable peeler, cutting crosswise into quarter inch slices, saving back the florets for another dish, another day. Place broccoli in a greased grill basket and cook over a hot fire. Grill for about 12 minutes, tossing and brushing with the cheese mixture the last six minutes of cooking. Serves 4.

Garlic Marinated Strip Steaks

4 Kansas City Strip steaks, one inch thick
2 cloves garlic, minced
1 tablespoon olive oil
4 to 6 fresh tarragon leaves, cut in pieces

Mix garlic, oil, and tarragon leaves together and coat each steak on both sides with the mixture. Place steaks in a glass baking dish, cover and let marinate in the refrigerator for two hours. Remove, and place directly on the grill over a hot fire. Grill for about seven minutes on each side for medium. Serves 4.

BRUSSELS SPROUTS

Sometime in the fourteenth century, a resident of Belgium got tired of eating the same old cabbages and thought up a way to produce miniaturized versions from one plant. I'm glad someone brought Brussels sprouts out of the Dark Ages because there's nothing I like more than their fat little heads picked fresh and grilled. If overcooked, their essence bleeds away, making them limp and soggy candidates for the compost heap.

The first time I grew Brussels sprouts I didn't know what to expect. I started with seedlings similar to that of cabbages and expected they would grow to a nice manageable size. I found out that even the so-called "dwarf" Jade Cross grows to a height of about two feet, with other varieties rising even higher. Perhaps it was too much rich compost or the fertile inner city soil, but my plants grew high enough to reach my waistline. This was fine with me because there was so much more to harvest.

Even if you don't like Brussels sprouts, plant a stalk anyway just to watch how it evolves. First the foliage leafs out on top, making it resemble an umbrella. Then sprouts begin to encircle the bottom of the stem and eventually spiral upward, making the plant look like a botanical specimen for aliens to take back to Andromeda Galaxy, rather than edible human fare.

Not only do these plants look weird, they are weird. They actually like frost. It's good for them. Their best and sweetest flavor comes after the first frost and you have to wait until then to harvest, or their taste is bitter.

Some gardeners cut off the bottom sprouts and then remove the leaves below to ensure uniform growth throughout the stalk. If you want the sprouts to mature at the same time, you can cut the top cluster of leaves about a month or so before harvesting. It's a good way to "top off" the plant and have a great dinner filled with these garden delights.

Brussels Sprouts
with Garlic Butter and Feta Cheese

1 1/2 pounds small Brussels sprouts, trimmed
2 tablespoons butter
1 teaspoon fresh garlic, minced
4 tablespoons fresh Feta cheese, crumbled
2 tablespoons water or milk (optional)
Double wooden skewers (soaked in water for 30 minutes)

Blanch Brussels sprouts until they are barely tender when pierced with a fork. Combine butter, garlic and cheese together in a saucepan and heat over a low fire until the mixture is smooth. Thread Brussels sprouts on skewers and brush with the warmed mixture, adding water or milk to thin, if needed. Place on grill over high heat and turn frequently, basting continuously with remaining mixture for about 8 to 10 minutes, or until the sprouts are tender. Serves 4.

Brussels Sprouts with Citrus Butter

2 cups small Brussels sprouts, trimmed
2 tablespoons butter, melted
2 tablespoons fresh orange juice
1 tablespoon fresh lemon juice
Double wooden skewers (soaked in water for 30 minutes)

Blanch Brussels spouts until they are barely tender when pierced with a fork. Combine butter, and juices together. Brush Brussels spouts with the mixture and thread on skewers. Grill over high heat for about 10 minutes, turning frequently and basting with remaining mixture, for about 8 to 10 minutes or until the sprouts are tender. Serves 4.

CARROTS

My worst school cafeteria experiences had to do with eating canned, frozen, or miserably overcooked carrots. Even today, just the thought of having to down those soggy, limp things makes me gag. I'm not sure why there is a tendency to desecrate this fabulous vegetable in such a way as to make it virtually inedible, especially when it's just as easy to eat it raw, steamed, or grilled.

Growing carrots requires suitable ground which has to be cultivated. My own soil is rather heavy, and so I have to work harder to give my carrots the light, fertile, and loamy ground they need. Many gardeners recommend making raised beds for carrots to improve the quality of the crop. Carrots will become malformed if they have to grow around obstructions like rocks, lumps, or buried treasure. I'll often mix radish and carrot seed together since the radishes pave the way for carrot growth by loosening the soil enough for the carrots to break through.

There are several carrot varieties from which to choose: some are long and tapered, others are short and round. There are also "finger" carrots, or baby carrot varieties that are also tasty. All are high in vitamin A and Beta Carotene which are good for you.

Carrots are at their best when picked young. Many people harvest them before they are fully grown. This is because the shorter the growing time, the sweeter the taste. Fresh carrots have such a sweet, delicious flavor that I have to stop myself from devouring them like candy when I'm preparing them for a salad. I also like fresh carrots steamed and drizzled with butter or glazed in orange-lemon ginger butter and served with grilled fish.

Glazed Carrots

1 pound small, slender carrots, trimmed, scraped, and cut into
   half-inch pieces
3 tablespoons butter
1 tablespoon brown sugar
1 tablespoon lemon juice
1 cup orange juice
1 tablespoon finely grated fresh ginger

In a large skillet over medium heat combine butter and brown sugar and stir until smooth. Add lemon juice, orange juice, and ginger. Toss the carrots in the mixture to glaze for about four minutes. Remove carrots from skillet and place remaining glaze mixture in a small dish for basting. Place carrots on grill topper over high heat, and baste frequently, turning often, until just tender—about 5-8 minutes. Serves 4.

Minted Baby Carrots

4 cups baby carrots
1/4 cup minced fresh mint
2 tablespoons butter, softened

Blanch carrots until they are barely tender when pierced with a fork. Combine mint and butter. Brush carrots with mixture and place on greased grill rack over high heat, turning frequently for about 15 to 20 minutes or until tender. Serves 4 to 6.

Stir-Grilled Vegetables with Island Marinade

8 to 10 slender carrots, scraped, and thinly sliced

2 large Portobello mushroom caps, thinly sliced

1/2 pound snow peas, cleaned and stems removed

1 medium leek, thinly sliced

3 peppers (1 red, 1 yellow, 1 green), cored, seeded, and sliced

Island Marinade

1 mango, peeled and diced

1 papaya, peeled and diced

1 orange, peeled and diced

1 tablespoon Key Lime juice

1 tablespoon lemon juice

1 tablespoon finely chopped cilantro

1 tablespoon finely chopped fresh mint leaves

1 tablespoon toasted sesame oil

Combine marinade ingredients. Pour over vegetables and let sit in the refrigerator for 30 minutes. Remove vegetables, setting marinade aside for basting. Grill peppers and carrots together in an oiled grill wok, over hot coals, for two minutes. Add additional vegetables, basting with remaining *Island Marinade,* and continue grilling for about 6 minutes, or until vegetables are tender. Serves 4 to 6.

Grilled Pork Tenderloin Kebobs—Southern Comfort Style

1 1/2 pounds pork tenderloin, trimmed and cubed

Marinade
1/3 cup olive oil
1/4 cup Southern Comfort
1 clove garlic, finely chopped
1/2 teaspoon dried rosemary
1/4 teaspoon salt
1/4 teaspoon freshly ground pepper
Grated zest of 1 orange
Juice of 1 orange

Combine marinade ingredients and pour over pork tenderloin cubes in glass dish. Cover and refrigerate for 2 hours. Remove meat from marinade and reserve liquid for basting. Skewer meat pieces and grill over a medium-hot fire for about 15 minutes, turning and basting with reserved marinade every three to four minutes until meat reaches desired doneness. Serves 4.

My personal preference for using Southern Comfort in a marinade is the result of a happy accident. I ran out of wine, and had an old bottle of Southern Comfort sitting on a basement shelf. In desperation I used it and to my surprise found the result so satisfying that I now prefer using this liqueur (once the favorite of '60s singer, Janis Joplin) in place of wine in some of my cooking.

CAULIFLOWER

Cauliflower is the whitest member of the *Brassica Oleracea* family of "cole crops" that includes such relatives as kohlrabi, broccoli, cabbage, and Brussels sprouts. All of these vegetables thrive well in cool, humid temperatures and fertile soil that has been dressed with nitrogen-rich organic material. If you've never grown cauliflower, check with a local nursery for varieties that do well in your area.

Both broccoli and cauliflower are the descendants of the wild cabbage and are similar in structure. Cauliflower, however, is the most delicate of the cabbage family and gets very stressed out in hot weather unless you cool it down with plenty of water and keep it well drained. On the other hand, temperatures lower than 44 degrees can stunt its growth.

Like a fair-haired woman that must shade her skin, the snow-white cauliflower doesn't like the hot sun on its head. I cover the head when it is still small by folding several of the plant's leaves over the crown and binding them together with twine or string. The leaves act as a sort of sunscreen, or hat, helping to maintain the pristine whiteness of the cauliflower and preserving its flavor.

Cauliflower is best when eaten fresh. It seems to like the cool of the morning, so I harvest it then, but once cut, it seems to have an aversion to cold. I don't like to refrigerate cauliflower, since its delicate taste quickly deteriorates and the longer it sits, the worse it gets. If you do have to store it, make sure it's not for any longer than four or five days.

Always inspect cauliflower closely if you're buying store-bought. If it looks discolored, or has brownish spots, avoid it. Look for cauliflower that is firm, with tight curds and fresh leaves. Some cooks add milk to the water when poaching cauliflower to keep the curds fresh tasting. I think boiling or poaching drains nutrients, so I don't do it unless the vegetable, itself, or a particular recipe, requires it. I eat cauliflower raw, steamed, or quick-grilled and serve it with butter and curry spices or lemon juice.

Grilled Cauliflower with Spicy Butter Sauce

    1 head cauliflower, cut into florets
    4 tablespoons butter
    1/4 teaspoon cinnamon
    1/4 teaspoon dried coriander
    1/2 teaspoon freshly grated ginger
    1/8 teaspoon saffron threads, crushed (optional)
    1/4 teaspoon ground cardamom
    1 tablespoon minced garlic

In a large skillet, cook butter over medium heat until golden brown. Add cinnamon, coriander, ginger, saffron, cardamom, and garlic and stir into a buttery sauce. Add cauliflower and coat the florets all over with sauce and cook for three to four minutes, stirring occasionally. With a slotted spoon, transfer cauliflower florets to grill topper, saving back any remaining sauce for basting. Grill vegetables over hot coals, basting and turning frequently. Cook for five minutes or until crunchy-tender, but not overcooked. Serves 4.

Minted Casablanca Chicken Strips

    1 1/2 pounds chicken breasts, skinned, boned, and cut into
        1-inch pieces
    2 tablespoons lime juice
    1/2 teaspoon salt
    1/4 cup plain yogurt (do not use fat free)
    4 cloves garlic, minced
    1 1/2 tablespoons ground coriander
    3 tablespoons chopped fresh mint

Blend lime juice, salt, yogurt, garlic, coriander and mint together in a large shallow dish. Add chicken and coat well. Cover and marinate for at least three hours in the refrigerator or overnight. Bring to room temperature prior to cooking. Place chicken in kebob baskets or thread on pre-soaked double wooden skewers. Grill over a hot fire, turning often for 7 to 10 minutes. Serves 4.

CORN

I didn't know what to expect the first time I grew corn, certainly not the wave of sugar-loving ants that made their way to the top of the tassel-waving cornstalks to drink in the plant's milky sweetness. When I saw these intrepid insects crawling all over the corn, I hosed them off. Then I figured that maybe they were supposed to be there for a reason, so now I leave them alone and we work in tandem to produce a nice harvest.

No matter what varieties you choose, corn needs warm weather, direct sunlight, and lots of fertilizer and water. Corn takes up a lot of space and produces only one or two ears per stalk, so you need ample room for planting. To ensure that it doesn't shade other vegetables, I either isolate it or put it at the north end of the garden plot.

The first time I planted corn, I put all the seeds in a straight line. Imagine my surprise when I grew pathetic-looking ears that would have been better buried than cooked. Now I sow seeds one to two inches deep and four inches apart, planting at least four adjacent rows of the same variety. Corn has a much better chance of developing when you place it side by side across from one another. This is because the wind-carried pollen can reach the neighboring stalks more easily as opposed to the missed opportunities that occur when corn is planted in one long linear column. I plant early, midseason, and late varieties together at the same time and, if I have room, I put in a late variety about three weeks later.

Patience is the key to producing good-tasting corn. Corn planted in May usually ripens in August, so don't jumpstart the process by sowing seed before the temperature of the soil is warm enough to ensure proper growth. Corn is a thirsty, greedy plant and needs plenty of water and nitrogen for it to flourish.

The right timing is essential to harvest corn. The trick is in the picking. Wait until the tassels turn brown and the tip of the husk is rounded. At this time the ear should feel solid and its kernels will be milky and ripe for grilling.

Naked Corn-in-the-Husk with Spicy Pepper

6 ears of corn
4 tablespoons unsalted butter, softened
1/2 teaspoon cayenne pepper (or to taste)
2 teaspoons finely minced garlic (optional)

Mix the softened butter with garlic and cayenne pepper and set aside. Peel back corn husks, taking care not to pull them off. Remove silks and pull husks back over corn, tying securely with string. Soak in cold water for 15 minutes. Remove from water and grill over high heat for 15 to 20 minutes turning often. Take corn off grill with tongs. Pull off leaves and brush the butter onto the corn, and serve. Serves 6.

ॐ

It may be corny to say this, but I am in love with this vegetable. There is nothing that equals it in sweetness (except for the asparagus green bean). Nestled in its own husk and brushed with butter, fresh-from-the-garden corn is remarkably flavorful and nutritious. Corn, also called maize, has been roasted by many cultures through the centuries including Native Americans who shared their harvests with the early Pilgrims. Some people prefer to spread each ear with flavored butter prior to grilling. If you want to try the merits of maize totally naked and unashamed (the corn, that is), I recommend grilling it first, then serving with seasoning of your choice such as cayenne-garlic butter. (You can always use leftovers, or grill some extra corn for use in the following recipe for Grilled Corn and Black Bean Salad*).*

Grilled Corn and Black Bean Salad

2 ears grilled corn (see *Naked Corn-in-the-Husk with Spicy Pepper*)

1 cup cooked black beans, drained and rinsed, if canned

1 small red bell pepper, peeled, cored, and seeded

3 tablespoons fresh lemon juice

1 garlic clove, minced

2 tablespoons chopped fresh cilantro

2 teaspoons chopped fresh tarragon

Salt and freshly ground pepper to taste

3 tablespoons olive oil

Using a sharp knife, cut the corn kernels from the cob. In a large bowl, combine the black beans, corn, and bell pepper. In a small bowl, whisk together the lemon juice, garlic, herbs, and salt and pepper. Add olive oil, blending well. Pour vinaigrette mixture over the corn and black bean salad, tossing well. Serve at room temperature, or chilled. Serves 6.

Grilled Corn Relish

3 cups grilled kernel corn

1 red onion, chopped

2 small jalapeno peppers, seeded and minced

4 cloves garlic, minced

2 tablespoons red pepper flakes

2 tablespoons each, dried thyme and chopped parsley

1/2 cup olive oil

1 1/2 cups white wine vinegar

1/2 cup sugar

Bring ingredients to a boil, stirring often. Cool slightly and serve at room temperature, or cool completely and bottle; refrigerate up to a week. Makes 6 cups.

Portobello Mushroom Mozzarella "Burgers"

4 large Portobello mushroom caps, about three inches in diameter
2 tablespoons olive oil
4 slices Mozzarella cheese
2 garlic cloves, minced (optional)
French bread or sesame seed hamburger buns

Cut off mushroom stems to ensure that the caps lie flat. Blend olive oil and garlic together. Brush on mushrooms. Place caps on grill, gill side down and cook over high heat for four minutes, turning occasionally to prevent them from charring. Turn caps gill side up and cook for another minute. Place Mozzarella cheese slices inside the caps. Close grill lid, and cook about one minute or until cheese is melted. Place mushrooms on bread and serve with your favorite garnishes. Serves 4.

Grilled Herbed Hamburgers

1 pound ground round or chuck
3 tablespoons onion, finely chopped
2 teaspoons fresh parsley, finely chopped
2 teaspoons fresh tarragon, finely chopped
1 egg, beaten
3 tablespoons Italian bread crumbs
4 hamburger buns

Place meat in medium sized bowl. Add onion, herbs, egg, and bread crumbs and mix together well. Divide into four patties and place on greased grill rack over medium high heat and cook for 5 minutes on each side, until the meat is crusty brown and cooked throughout. Serve on toasted hamburger buns with your favorite garnishes. Serves 4.

EGGPLANT

One of the most interesting plants to cultivate in the garden is eggplant. These slow-growing vegetables need about four months to reach maturity from seed. Like its relatives, the tomato and pepper, eggplant is really a fruit, the most common of which is the purple variety. I usually set the plants out in spring about two feet apart because if the eggplant does decide to expand, it will spread out and get so heavy with fruit that it may need staking.

I never know from year to year if I'm going to get a crop or not. Fortunately, since I do not base my sole income on the erratic whims of nature, I can afford to play a little. When nighttime temperatures reach at least 50 degrees, I put it in the ground. An accidental dip into the '40s can wreak havoc on eggplant, weakening it to the point where it can be affected by blight.

Even so, eggplants may still thrive. Last year I thought my crop was gone. The plant looked skeletal and ready to die. Yet, I couldn't bring myself to pull it up. I kept thinking, what if a miracle would happen and I could get one lousy little eggplant after all? I still held out hope. Sure enough, as decimated as they were, the plants began to produce fruit in late summer, generating enough eggplant offspring to keep me grilling through September.

I am merely the gardener, so I don't profess to understand the inner workings of nature, nor can I fathom its secrets. All I do is stick stuff in the ground and water it. I let it do what it does best and try not to bother it too much, since eggplant, like other vegetables has its own way of doing things.

All I know is that there is something very exciting about holding this shiny, delicate fruit in my hand. From a watercolorist's standpoint, the shape and color of an eggplant, framed by leaves and foliage, is most intriguing. Sometimes I think I'd almost rather paint it than eat it, but I know that I must harvest it before it is fully grown, to get the best taste for grilling.

I clip the stem cleanly with scissors. The more I pick, the more the eggplant seems stimulated to generate new fruit. This is fine with me because I never get tired of eating it or giving it away to friends and family who love receiving this unusual garden gift.

Grilled Eggplant
with Olive Oil and Oven-Dried Tomatoes

2 small eggplants
3 tablespoons *Grilled Oven-Dried Tomatoes* (see recipe p.70)
1/2 cup extra virgin olive oil
1 clove garlic, finely minced
2 tablespoons dried oregano, crumbled

Slice the ends off the eggplants, but do not peel. Cut lengthwise into 1/4 inch slices. Lightly salt, and place in colander and let drain for at least 30 minutes to remove excess water. Pat dry. Combine oil, garlic, and oregano. Brush mixture on both sides of the eggplant slices. Place on grill rack and cook directly on the grill over medium high heat, turning once, until tender, about 10 minutes. Brush on *Grilled Oven-Dried Tomatoes* the last two minutes of cooking time. Serves 4.

৪৯

If you're in the mood for something simple and meatless, put a side of eggplant together with a pasta dish, and you've got a great Italian-inspired meal that is sure to tempt every palate. Small eggplants are good for grilling and are less bitter than older large ones. It's important to allow eggplant to "weep" before you cook it. By allowing it to release excess moisture, eggplant will not absorb as much grease, and it will taste less bitter. Some cooks cover the eggplant slices with paper towels and place a heavy skillet on top to make sure all the juices get squished out.

FENNEL

As both an herb and a vegetable, fennel wins hands-down as a champion of diversity. I use the seeds not only for their special anise flavor, but also as an aid to digestion, especially after a large, heavy meal. Fennel is also a good breath sweetener. Eating a few seeds before you have to come into close proximity with others, can considerably improve your ability to make a good impression.

The sweet licorice taste of fennel is what makes it a prime choice of cooks who use the stalks, fronds, seeds, and bulbs in salads, pasta, rice dishes, and marinades.

Fennel from the garden tastes so much better than the supermarket variety because it keeps its fresh-picked intensity. The fronds resemble dill, but the similarity ends there, for taste clearly separates the two.

Bulbing or Florence fennel is priced by Italian cooks for its bulb, stalks and seeds. Since all parts of fennel are edible, you can harvest the leaves and fronds as the bulb is growing. The young stalks, when eaten raw, can be used like celery. Many gardeners plant fennel as a late winter or early spring crop, since fennel seems to like cooler weather. If you sow seed about ten weeks before the first fall frost, you should get good-sized bulbs. Keep the plant watered to prevent it from bolting.

If you plant fennel in spring, it may bolt in the summer heat. It's best to plant it in late August or about two months or so before the first frost. Make sure your soil is rich enough to produce big bulbs and water it in dry weather so the plant won't go to seed.

Fennel can be braised, sauteed, and grilled, or roasted with chicken, sauteed with onion, and scooped out and stuffed with seafood. Personally I like fennel on the grill, basted with lemon and herbs, and sprinkled with Italian cheese, and served with fresh grilled fish accompanied by dollops of chervil butter.

Lemon-Basted Fennel
with Tarragon and Romano Cheese

2 fennel bulbs, rinsed, quartered and trimmed of tops and stalks

Baste
1/2 cup olive oil
juice of one lemon
zest of one lemon
1 clove garlic, minced
3 tablespoons minced fresh tarragon
2 tablespoons butter, melted
Grated Pecorino Romano Cheese

Blanch fennel for 8 minutes, or until tender enough to pierce with a sharp knife. Drain and cool. Combine olive oil, juice, zest, garlic, and tarragon and pour over the fennel. Marinate in the refrigerator for four hours. Remove the fennel, pour baste into a separate bowl, adding the butter to mixture. Place the fennel on a grill rack over high heat, turning often and brushing with baste continuously until fennel is tender inside and outside, about 10 to 15 minutes. Sprinkle grated cheese over the fennel. Serves 4.

Grilled Catfish with Dill

4 farm-raised catfish fillets
4 tablespoons olive oil
2 medium sized bunches of fresh dill, coarsely chopped
2 tablespoons butter

Brush fish with oil, sprinkle with dill and place on a greased grill rack. Grill for about 10 minutes, turning once. Top with butter. Serves 4.

GARLIC AND SHALLOTS

Growing garlic is a no-brainer. You put bulbs in the ground in fall, cover with a little soil, let it sit through winter, and when the tops wither and brown, you'll be able to harvest a plant that, when eaten raw, will make your breath powerful enough to ward off vampires. Garlic, also called the "stinking rose," has a much more intense flavor and odor than do the milder-flavored shallots which taste like a cross between leeks and garlic.

Garlic and shallots are like an old married couples who have grown so used to each others smell and foibles that they enjoy each others company. Garlic bulbs can be divided into cloves and set about eight inches apart. Plant garlic close to the soil surface, cover with well-rotted manure, and harvest about a week after the tops or leaves wither and die.

Shallots, like garlic, are planted from cloves in spring or fall. To harvest shallots or garlic, pull up the clumps, separate the bulbs, and let the bulbs "cure" for about a month in a dark, dry place.

Used in French cuisine, the shallot has become a household staple of gourmet cooks. Shallots meld beautifully with wine, butter, and lemon juice and adding shallots to a dish that calls for onions can impart an even more unique taste. Shallots don't come cheap. So you might as well grow your own if you're going to use them a lot in your cooking.

As for garlic, according its herbalist advocates, it is a universal remedy that can reduce high blood pressure, cure cancer, and aid in digestion. Old World Europeans festooned their doorposts with garlic to keep away evil spirits. I actually gave this a try myself. I hung a garland of garlic bulbs on my screen door, posting a note alongside that read "no religious solicitation, surveys, sales, or evil spirits welcome here."

Alas, this ancient method of repelling unwanted guests didn't work for me. I have gone back to using garlic in the kitchen, instead, grilling it alone or in tandem with anything that clucks, moos, oinks, swims, or grows in the garden.

Smokey Garlic-Walnut Pesto

2 large garlic heads, unpeeled with papery skin removed
1/4 cup chopped walnuts
2 cups loosely packed fresh basil leaves
1/2 cup freshly grated Parmesan cheese
2 tablespoons freshly grated Pecorino Romano cheese
1/3 cup extra-virgin olive oil
Salt and pepper to taste

Place garlic on oil-coated vegetable rack or grill rack. Grill over high heat until soft, about 8 minutes. Leave room beside the rack to add a medium piece of foil wrap for grilling walnuts. Place walnuts on foil over high heat and grill until toasty brown. Remove garlic and walnuts and let cool. Squeeze out garlic pulp and place in a food processor along with walnuts, basil, and cheeses and blend well. With the machine running, add the olive oil slowly and process to a smooth consistency. Let stand for five minutes. Store in air tight glass jar, topped with olive oil. Makes about 1/2 to 3/4 cup.

❦

The taste of grilled garlic is totally awesome. It doesn't have the sharp bite that raw garlic has. Used as a spread, grilled garlic can be mashed and pureed and slathered on bread, added to soups, dressings, and other fine things to eat. Blended into a pesto, it can be spread on a chunk of Italian bread or served with pasta.

Grilled Garlic Dip with Shallots

2 large garlic heads, unpeeled with papery skin removed
1 8-ounce package lowfat cream cheese
1 cup lowfat sour cream
1 tablespoon shallots, peeled and minced
1/2 teaspoon fresh lemon juice
Salt and freshly ground pepper to taste

Place garlic on oil-coated vegetable rack or grill rack. Grill over high heat until soft, about 8 minutes. In a food processor combine grilled garlic pulp, cream cheese, and sour cream and process until smooth. In a glass bowl combine garlic mixture with scallions, lemon juice and salt and pepper. Serve with your favorite crackers as a dip. Makes about 2 cups.

Grilled Shallots with Tarragon Butter

1 pound shallots, peeled
Tarragon Butter
Salt and freshly ground pepper to taste

Brush grill topper with oil to prevent sticking. Place shallots directly on grill topper over high heat. Turn them occasionally until they are evenly browned all over, about 6 to 8 minutes. Brush with *Tarragon Butter* and serve. Serves 4.

Tarragon Butter
4 ounces (1 stick) unsalted butter, softened
2 tablespoons fresh chopped tarragon
1 tablespoon tarragon vinegar
Dash of Tabasco

Mix butter with remaining ingredients. Place in the middle of a sheet of foil or plastic wrap and roll into a cylinder. Wrap and chill until ready to serve. Freeze any remaining butter in foil wrap for later use.

Grilled Scallops

1 1/4 pound sea scallops, rinsed
Tarragon Butter

Marinade
2 teaspoons finely chopped shallots
2 teaspoons finely chopped garlic
1 1/2 teaspoons Dijon mustard
1/3 cup white wine
1/3 cup fresh lemon juice
1/2 cup olive oil

Combine marinade ingredients. Add scallops to marinade and toss until thoroughly coated. Marinate for 30 minutes. Remove scallops from marinade and pour remaining liquid into a saucepan. Arrange scallops on a grill topper, keeping them flat. Cook for about three minutes, basting with *Tarragon Butter* until scallops can be lifted from grill without sticking. Turn over and cook for 2 more minutes. Bring reserved marinade to a boil and simmer for 2 minutes. Arrange scallops on a platter and spoon marinade over all. Serve immediately Serves 4.

Grilled Chicken Wings

3 pounds chicken wings
1/2 cup Dijon mustard
2 teaspoons olive oil
4 cloves garlic, minced
1/4 cup soy sauce
1/2 teaspoon ground ginger

Cut chicken wings into three pieces and discard the tips. Combine other ingredients into a large bowl. Add wing pieces and stir to coat well. Cover and let stand for 45 minutes in the refrigerator. Place wing pieces on the grill and brush with remaining mustard mixture. Grill over medium-hot fire for 15 to 20 minutes, turning once. Serves 6 to 8.

GREEN BEANS

It's mid-July and my green beans emerge from their beautiful purple blossoms, like graceful branches reaching upward. I admit a fondness for both bushy snap beans and pole beans, but the only pole bean I grow is the "asparagus" green bean which is my true love. This long, pencil-thin bean is actually an oriental variety of cowpea or field pea called dow gauk. These beans neither resemble asparagus, nor taste like conventional green beans. When eaten raw, they impart an intensely sweet flavor that reminds me of honeysuckle.

I harvest the asparagus green beans when they fit the length of my hand, from the edge of my wrist to the end of my middle finger. Otherwise the beans will keep on growing, sometimes to a startling length of two feet!

Green beans are easily started directly from seed. All that's required for their growth is water, good dirt, and sunshine. Pole beans, if left to their own devices, become unmanageable beanstalks, so you need to stake them and provide them with support. Bush beans, on the other hand, usually grow no taller than two feet. For my asparagus green beans I tie poles together in tent-like fashion and plant about five beans around each pole. By the time I finish my May planting, the back yard looks like a tepee village.

In June pole beans sprout and become stalks from which vines and blossoms emerge. Upward they go, sending out delicate tendrils that wind together in great profusion. In July, the green beans suddenly materialize. Asparagus green beans are particularly sugary and attract ants. The creatures arrive in hordes so thick I have to hose them off before I can pick the beans. However, I don't mind sharing because there always seems to be enough for both the ants and me.

If there's room, I make successive plantings of pole and bush beans in May, June, and plant again in early fall. Beans love nitrogen, so I give them plenty of it. I pick them daily, before they get too big, and sometimes down them on the spot if I can't wait long enough to grill them.

Grilled Beans with Lemon Verbena Pesto

1 1/2 pounds asparagus green beans (or regular green beans)
2 teaspoons olive oil
4 tablespoons *Lemon Verbena Pesto*

Brush beans with olive oil and stir-grill for 5 to 8 minutes in an oiled grill wok until tender. Remove and toss with 2 tablespoons *Lemon Verbena Pesto*.
Serves 2-4.

Lemon Verbena Pesto
1 cup fresh lemon verbena leaves
2 garlic cloves
1/4 cup grated Parmesan cheese
1/4 cup pine nuts
1/2 cup olive oil
Salt and freshly-ground pepper to taste

Combine lemon verbena, garlic, cheese, pine nuts and puree in a food processor. Slowly add the olive oil with the processor running. Season to taste with salt and pepper and process until blended into a smooth paste. Makes about 1 cup.

ℰ౨

Lemon Verbena Pesto is one of my favorite pesto variations. You can also substitute fresh basil, oregano, tarragon, or other herbs.

Grilled Green Beans with Walnuts

3/4 pound young thin green beans, trimmed
2 teaspoons olive oil
1/4 cup toasted walnuts, finely chopped
2 teaspoons walnut oil
2 teaspoons fresh lemon juice
Freshly ground pepper

Brush beans with oil and stir-grill for 5 to 8 minutes in an oiled grill wok until tender. Remove and toss with walnuts, walnut oil, and lemon juice. Season with pepper and serve immediately. Serves 2 to 4.

Grilled Poached Salmon with White Wine and Herbs

4 (8-ounce) salmon fillets
4 teaspoons melted butter
1/4 cup parsley, finely chopped
1 leek, trimmed, peeled, and finely chopped
5 mushrooms, finely chopped
4 tablespoons dry white wine
1/2 teaspoon rosemary
4 large pieces of foil wrap

Brush both sides of fillets with melted butter and place skin-side down on foil wrap. Distribute parsley, chopped leek, and mushrooms evenly over fillets, and add 1 tablespoon wine to each. Sprinkle 1/8 teaspoon rosemary across the tops. Tightly wrap each fillet in foil. Grill foil packets for approximately 15 minutes over medium hot coals. Place a packet on each of four dinner plates and serve. Serves 4.

Herb-and-Honey Grilled Chicken Breasts

4 whole chicken breasts, skinned, boned and split (about 1
    pound each)
2 tablespoons olive oil
Freshly ground pepper
Assortment of fresh herb sprigs (rosemary, thyme, tarragon, fennel)
2 tablespoons honey

Lightly oil and pepper chicken. Place herbs inside a herb grill rack and set over a medium hot fire. Place chicken on herb rack and grill for 12 minutes, turning chicken once, until golden brown and firm to the touch. Drizzle honey over the chicken pieces the last five minutes of cooking. Serves 4 to 6.

જી

This is one way to grill chicken. You can also baste it with Italian herb salad dressing, brush it with flavored butter, or make up your own aromatic rub using your favorite fresh herbs. Just before you take it off the grill, brush it with your favorite barbecue sauce.

GREENS

The French have mixed their greens together for years. The "mesclun" combination is not only beautiful to behold, but tastes great, too. Best of all greens are so easy to grow that even beginners can produce wondrous leafy vegetables from seed.

In the summer, you'll do much better growing mesclun yourself rather than paying high prices for it at the store. Relatives of these lettuces—the once-lowly collards and mustard greens—are all the rage at upscale gourmet groceries that sell cooked greens by the pound. Because I do not have boundless space in my city garden, I have to concentrate solely on those greens which I like to eat and that are easy to grow from seed or as seedlings. These include collards, kale, mustard greens, bok choy (an Asian cabbage), spinach, and sorrel, plus a mesclun mix of arugula, chervil, and radicchio.

I limit my other lettuces to loose leaf, Bibb, and romaine. As for iceberg lettuce, I don't waste my time. Radicchio, endive, and escarole are forms of chicory that take well to grilling. These are also cool weather crops that grow like lettuce. To grow lettuce, all you have to do is follow the instructions on the seed packet. If you're a busy person, stick with those that aren't delicate and don't require daily devotion. Plant the seeds in early spring, making sure the soil is fertile and well drained. Water, thin out the young shoots (I consume them on the spot), and in a few weeks you'll have lettuce. Instructions on the seed packet will tell you when and how to plant. You can repeat sowings at two week intervals until late May. In mid-summer, lettuce has heat stroke, goes kaput, and turns into fish food. In late August, I plant again for a fall crop.

Other greens to grill include mustard greens and bok choy which can be grown from seedlings. Thin out the mustard greens when they're about five inches high. The whole plant can be harvested in a little over a month, or you can let it stay in the ground and use the leaves for steaming. Bok choy, can be planted in spring and harvested in about two months. The smaller the head, the better for grilling.

Endive and Escarole with Olive Oil and Feta Cheese

2 small heads of endive
2 small heads of escarole
1/4 cup olive oil
1/2 cup feta cheese, crumbled
Salt and pepper to taste

Trim leaves from each head, wash, and drain thoroughly. Brush well with olive oil. Place endive and escarole on well oiled grill rack over mesquite chips on a hot grill and cover with grill top for 5 to 8 minutes. Turn, brush with oil and grill until tender and browned, about another minute or two. Top with crumbled feta cheese, sprinkle with seasonings and serve. Serves 4.

Garlic-Buttered Bok Choy with Soy Sauce and Ginger

2 small heads bok choy
1/4 cup unsalted butter
2 tablespoons olive oil
2 teaspoons soy sauce
1 garlic clove, minced
2 teaspoons minced fresh ginger

Wash the bok choy, trim bases, and cut in half lengthwise. Blend together butter, olive oil, soy sauce, garlic and ginger. Brush bok choy with mixture. Place on oiled grill rack, cut side down over medium heat for 10 minutes. Turn over, basting with mixture until heads are tender, about 10 minutes. Serves 4.

Penne Pasta in Tomato and Basil Sauce with Grilled Greens

1 pound penne pasta, cooked al dente
2 tablespoons extra virgin olive oil
4 cloves garlic, crushed
4 ripe Italian plum tomatoes, peeled and diced
1 cup chopped fresh basil
Salt and freshly ground pepper
3/4 cup freshly grated Parmesan cheese
Grilled Greens

Saute the oil and garlic together for a minute, add tomatoes and basil and cook for 8 minutes stirring often with a wooden spoon. Place the drained pasta in a bowl, pour the sauce over it and mix together thoroughly. Add the *Grilled Greens* and toss well. Sprinkle with seasonings and top with grated Parmesan cheese. Serves 4.

Grilled Greens
1 1/2 pounds mustard greens, spinach, chard, and/or
    collards, washed and thoroughly dried
3 tablespoons olive oil

Wash greens thoroughly to remove all dirt, and pat dry. Brush leaves and stalks with oil and toss in a grill wok, turning frequently with long-handled tongs or wooden paddles until greens are browned, wilted and tender, about 10 minutes. Serves 4.

Grilled Radicchio with Garlic-Braised Mushrooms

  1 head radicchio
  1 pound large button mushrooms, washed, dried, and stems
    removed
  1/2 cup olive oil
  1 clove garlic, crushed

Trim base of radicchio head, leaving leaves attached. Slice in half lengthwise, rinse, drain, and pat dry. Mix together olive oil and garlic. Brush radicchio and mushrooms with oil mixture, coating well. Place vegetables in a grill rack over medium hot fire, turning occasionally, until lightly browned, about 3 to 5 minutes per side for radicchio; about 10 minutes for mushrooms. Cool to room temperature. Serves 2 to 4.

Grilled Ham Slice with Brown Sugar and Butter

  1 ham slice (1 1/2 inches thick)
  3 tablespoons brown sugar, packed
  2 tablespoons melted butter
  1 tablespoon lemon juice
  1 tablespoon dry mustard
  1 teaspoon orange peel
  dash paprika

Combine all ingredients except for ham and set aside. Trim outside fat from ham, and place on grill about 5 inches above coals. Brown on one side and then turn. Begin basting and cook about 20 minutes, continuing to turn and baste frequently. Serves 2.

LEEKS

Believe it or not, leeks—although seemingly fragile—are actually hardier than onions. Historically speaking, their use dates back to ancient Egypt and Rome. Leeks have been used in European cuisine for centuries and are prized by those who love the sweet mild flavor.

If anyone asks you to take a leek, do not hesitate. In fact, take several leeks, if you can afford to do so. Like shallots, leeks are a variation on the onion family and I prefer them to scallions because of the subtle, yet intense flavor they impart to my cooking. Leeks have a flavor any way you prepare them, be it wood smoked, poached, sauteed, julienned, braised in cream, or grilled. The taste of grilled leeks alone or in combination with other food, is something to be savored. Many cooks use leeks in soups and stews in combination with potatoes or other vegetables.

Like onions, leeks need a lot of sun, water, and well-drained soil that is enriched with organic matter. Seeds are slow on the uptake, requiring two to three weeks to germinate. Some varieties are overwintering and can be harvested in spring. Others are planted in spring and harvested in autumn—some even as late as Thanksgiving. You can sow seed directly in the soil after the last frost and dig up when the stem diameter reaches an inch around (about 130 days). Thin the seedlings to about six inches apart and, as the leeks grow, put a mound of soil around the stems to keep the stem base white and mild. Keep increasing the height of the soil around to cover the base of the plant as it develops and be sure the dirt is kept away from the leaf joints.

When you're ready to prepare them, remove the dirt, cut off the stringy root, and any excess leaves. Leave at least a couple of inches of green to eat because it tastes so great.

Mesquite-Flavored Pork Patties with Grilled Leeks

1 pound lean ground pork
3/4 finely grated Italian bread crumbs
3/4 cup grated Parmesan cheese
3 cloves garlic, crushed
3 eggs
1/2 teaspoon salt
1/4 teaspoon pepper
1 teaspoon dried sage
1/2 teaspoon dried rosemary
Grilled Leeks

Make a well in the middle of the meat. Add bread crumbs, cheese, garlic, eggs, spices and herbs and mix thoroughly. Mold meat into four 3/4-inch thick patties. Grill pork patties over hot coals with moistened mesquite chips added, until meat is very well done and there is no pink in the middle (about 5 to 7 minutes per side). Place *Grilled Leeks* on top of each pattie and serve on grilled hamburger buns with garnishes of your choice. Serves 4.

Grilled Leeks
3 leeks, about 1 inch around
2 teaspoons olive oil

Trim roots and leaves from leeks. Slice down the middle, separate and wash thoroughly to remove any dirt or sand. Drain, and pat dry. Slice into thin 2-inch lengths. Brush with oil and place on grill rack. Grill leeks over hot coals with moistened mesquite chips added, turning frequently, until brown and tender (about 6 to 8 minutes). Serves 4.

ONIONS AND SCALLIONS

What's bulbous, stinky, and responsive to rotted manure? No, it is not a politician; it's an onion. A couple of bushels of organic matter per hundred square feet can give you some really nice onions. Finicky gardeners will not use onion sets, because the taste is strong and the odor, pungent. However, sets are the easiest to handle and produce onions within a month after planting. For green onions, plant the sets a couple of inches apart to a depth of one to two inches. For bigger bulbs, keep the sets close to the surface, about three inches apart.

Onion seeds require more time, patience, and care initially but you will find more seed varieties available than sets, including the sweeter, milder onions. Wait until the temperature reaches at least 65 degrees to plant the seeds and remember that onions need a lot of water, so your soil needs to be well drained and preferably alkaline, rather than acid. Sow the seed in half-inch deep furrows and after the onions are established, thin them to an inch apart for scallions, and three to five inches apart for larger bulbs.

Some gardeners plant radishes on either side of the onion rows as an organic preventive for pests such as maggots which can burrow into bulbs and destroy them.

Onions can be easily crowded out by weeds, so be merciless and yank out anything that doesn't go well with hamburgers. When the onion tops start to yellow, fold the leaves over and lay them flat, and let the onions sit in the ground for about three weeks or until the leaves wither. Dig up the onions carefully and lay them outside on paper bags in a shady spot to cure for another couple of weeks. After this, use them in soups, stews, or on the grill to add unique flavor to your meals.

Grilled Sliced Red Onions

1/2 cup olive oil
3 tablespoons Dijon mustard
2 teaspoons Balsamic vinegar
1 tablespoon fresh parsley, chopped
3 large red onions, cut into 1/2-inch slices

Combine oil, mustard, vinegar, and parsley and set mixture aside. Arrange onion slices on an oiled grill rack, and grill over a hot fire, turning and basting several times with the mixture, for about 10 minutes, or until tender and brown. Serves 6.

Key Lime Pompano

4 (8-ounce) pompano fillets
3 tablespoons vegetable oil
Salt and freshly cracked pepper to taste
1/4 cup extra-virgin olive oil
4 teaspoons Key Lime juice
2 tablespoons chopped parsley

Rub fillets with oil and season with salt and pepper. Place fillets skin side up on a grill topper and grill over medium-hot fire for 4 minutes. Turn over and cook for 3 minutes more, until fish is opaque all the way through. Remove fillets from grill, drizzle them with olive oil and pour 1 teaspoon of Key Lime juice over each. Sprinkle with chopped parsley. Serves 4.

❦

If pompano is not available, you may substitute tilapia, walleye pike, or mahi-mahi.

Grilled Garden Onions

4 whole fresh garden onions
1/3 cup olive oil
1 tablespoon balsamic vinegar
1 tablespoon minced fresh tarragon
Salt and freshly ground pepper to taste
2 teaspoons unsalted butter

Combine oil, vinegar, tarragon, and seasonings. Cut tops and bottoms of each onion and peel. Coat onions thoroughly with mixture. Place 1/2 teaspoon of butter on top of each onion, and wrap each onion tightly in foil wrap. Place directly on the coals over high heat until tender, brown, and sizzling hot (about 20 to 30 minutes). Remove from foil and serve. Serves 4.

Scallion Stuffed Italian Sausage

8 large Italian pork sausages
2 tablespoons Dijon mustard
6 to 8 scallions, peeled, washed, and sliced lengthwise into
    strips

With a sharp knife, cut a long slit about three quarters of the way through one side of each sausage. Cover the cut surface with mustard and stuff with scallion strips, pressing in firmly. Seal sausages shut with toothpicks to hold them together. Cook over a hot fire for 15 minutes, turning occasionally. Serves 4 to 6.

Grilled Onions and Tomatoes in Basil Vinaigrette

1 1/2 pounds Italian plum tomatoes, cut into slices
1 1/2 pounds red or sweet onions, cut into wedges
2 tablespoons olive oil
4 to 6 cups mesclun mix
Basil Vinaigrette

Toss tomatoes with 1/2 cup *Basil Vinaigrette* and set aside for one hour. Brush onion wedges with oil and place on greased grill rack over hot fire and grill for 10 minutes. Turn, brush with oil again, and grill for an additional 8 minutes or until onions are tender and golden. Arrange mesclun mix on four salad plates. Top with tomatoes and onions. Drizzle remaining vinaigrette over the salad. Sprinkle with seasonings and serve. Serves 4.

Basil Vinaigrette
1 garlic clove, peeled
1 cup fresh basil leaves
2 tablespoons Balsamic vinegar
6 tablespoons olive oil
Salt and freshly ground pepper

Combine garlic, basil, vinegar, and olive oil in a food processor until smooth. Season with salt and pepper. Makes about 1 cup.

PEAS

The old shell game doesn't apply for some peas which can stay right in the pod to be enjoyed. There are several varieties of peas. Edible pod peas are stringless and can be eaten like green beans when young, or you can let the peas swell in the pod and eat them when they mature. Shell peas are varieties that you shell and eat when the peas fill the pod. Snow peas have small flat pods that are good for stir-grilling. Snap peas need the strings removed before eating. Immature snap pea pods can be eaten whole or you can wait until they mature and shell them.

Stir-grilled alone or with other vegetables, crunchy and delicious pea pods are tasty, but costly at the grocery store. I prefer growing them myself in the summer since the freshness of garden-picked varieties far surpasses those that sit on the shelf for some time.

Peas like cool weather and wilt in temperatures above 80 degrees, so I plant them in early spring, usually about a month and a half before the last frost date. As a would-be watercolorist, I watch the progress of my peas and paint my observations. As time passes, the supporting leaves and tendrils wrap themselves delicately around poles and trellises, giving the garden a burst of sun-flecked greenery and beautiful tiny flowers from which the pods emerge.

The plants are almost too pretty to eat, but nevertheless I get impatient to pop the peas in my mouth. I plant them in two to three week intervals for maximum eating. Before sowing, I sometimes soak the seeds overnight in water for faster germination.

Peas should be planted about an inch deep and topped with rich organic matter, but be sure you don't have too much nitrogen in your soil or you'll get more foliage than peas. Also be watchful that the soil is warm because overwatering cold soil can cause peas to rot. Boost the yield, by dressing the peas with low-nitrogen fertilizer when the plants are about a half a foot high. If you plant in early spring and all goes well, you can harvest in early summer. Pick the pods right before cooking for the freshest, sweetest flavor.

Italian-Style Snow Peas with Peppers

1/2 pound snow peas
3 peppers (1 red, 1 yellow, 1 orange), julienned
2 teaspoons olive oil
2 teaspoons Balsamic vinegar
1/4 teaspoon sugar

Rinse and dry peas; combine with peppers. Combine oil, vinegar, and sugar and pour over vegetables in a glass bowl. Marinate for 2 hours in the refrigerator. Brush a grill rack with oil, place vegetables on top in a single layer and cook for a minute over medium hot coals. Turn with a spatula and cook for another 30 seconds. Serves 4 to 6.

Stir-Grilled Shrimp and Sugarsnap Peas

1 pound shrimp, cleaned, peeled, and deveined
1/2 pound sugarsnap peas, cleaned and stems removed
12 cherry tomatoes
1/2 red onion, sliced

Marinade
1/4 cup soy sauce
1/4 cup rice wine vinegar
2 tablespoons honey
4 cloves garlic, minced
1 teaspoon ground ginger
1 teaspoon toasted sesame oil

Combine marinade ingredients in a glass bowl. Add shrimp, peas, tomatoes, and onions, and marinate for 30 minutes or more. Pour shrimp mixture into a well-greased grill wok over the sink and partially drain liquid. Place wok over hot coals. Using large wooden spoons, stir-grill shrimp and vegetables for 6 to 8 minutes. Move wok to indirect heat side of grill, close lid, and cook for 4 to 5 minutes more. Serves 4.

PEPPERS

Peppers come in all sizes from long and skinny to cone-shaped, round, and crinkly. The shades range from banana yellow and rosy red to deep chocolate, and bright green. They can be mild and sweet or hot and spicy, depending on your taste.

Peppers are easy to grow, as long as you follow the rules. Don't plant peppers when it's cold and windy, or when the soil is still frigid and damp. That's pretty much it, except for picking pests off a peck of peppers now and then. Aphids love them as much as humans and you can dust with pyrethrum, a preferred favorite of organic gardeners, to control them.

If it is too hot or too cold, the plants won't form fruit. But once the weather is warm, the fruit will start to appear. I've gotten impatient and planted peppers too soon and, for my efforts, received a lot of leafy foliage and no peppers at all.

On other frustrating occasions, when I'm about to tear out plants with nothing but stunted little green thingies on them, the peppers go bonzo, and go into production full blast. Perhaps it's the tone of voice when I threaten them with death, or maybe it's because they really like me—whatever the reason—the peppers usually do very well by early autumn, giving me a colorful crop if I let them.

I often leave green peppers in the ground to ripen fully and turn red or gold—usually in late summer or early fall. Although I am not that fond of raw green peppers, I love the taste of them grilled. I put them on the fire unpeeled, quartered and seeded, and serve them as a summer appetizer, charred skin and all.

I usually plant several kinds of peppers including Golden Bell, Gypsy Hybrid, Purple Bell, Sweet Banana Peppers, Sweet Chocolate, Chocolate Bell, and Patio Bell, a dwarf sweet pepper. These have maturity dates that range from 60 to 80 days.

For those who prefer hot peppers and want to create the feeling of a blazing inferno in their mouths, I recommend Anaheim Hot, jalapeno and serrano varieties.

Depending on your time, you can start your peppers from seed, or grow them from seedlings. There are so many pepper varieties now at local greenhouses that, for many busy people, seedlings are the answer.

Hot and Spicy Grilled Peppers

3 large red bell peppers, cored, seeded and quartered
1 long Anaheim chile pepper, whole
4 cherry chili peppers, whole
4 fresh jalapeno peppers, whole
1 clove garlic, crushed
1/4 cup olive oil
Salt and freshly ground pepper to taste

Mix olive oil and garlic together and coat vegetables. Brush grill rack with oil and grill peppers over medium high heat, turning often to cook evenly, until lightly charred, about 6 to 9 minutes. Sprinkle with seasoning to taste. Serves 2 to 4.

This recipe comes from my cousin Susie in California.

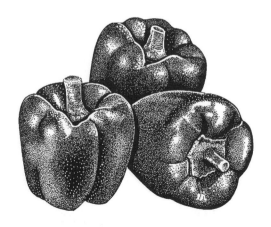

Grilled Pepper Medley

4 peppers (1 red, 1 yellow, 1 chocolate, 1 green), cored, seeded,
   and quartered
1 onion, peeled and quartered
2 tablespoons olive oil
2 tablespoons freshly chopped oregano
Salt and freshly ground pepper to taste

Combine peppers and onion; place on oil-coated grill rack. Grill 8 to 10 minutes, turning frequently, until pepper skins are smokey and charred and onions are slightly charred and tender. Toss with oregano and seasonings. Drizzle with oil, mixing well. Serves 4.

Grilled Duck Breast with Red Pepper Butter

4 duck breasts
Olive oil
Salt and freshly ground pepper to taste
Red Pepper Butter

Coat duck breasts with olive oil and season with salt and pepper. Grill for 10 minutes over a medium hot fire, turning once for medium-rare. Serve with a tablespoon of *Red Pepper Butter.* Serves 4.

Red Pepper Butter
1 stick unsalted butter, softened
2 tablespoons finely chopped grilled red pepper
3 tablespoons minced fresh chives
2 teaspoons freshly grated lime zest
1 tablespoon teriyaki sauce

Mix softened butter with ingredients. Place butter in the middle of a sheet of waxed paper and shape into a roll, about an inch around. Refrigerate for at least two hours prior to using. Freeze any remaining butter for later use.

Stir-Grilled Chicken
with Tangerine and Ginger Sauce

4 skinless, boneless chicken breast halves, cut in 1-inch cubes
2 red peppers, peeled, cored, and sliced

Tangerine and Ginger Sauce
2 teaspoons olive oil
1/2 cup orange juice
2 tangerines, peeled, seeded, and chopped
1 large clove garlic, minced
2 teaspoons freshly grated ginger root

Combine sauce ingredients and pour over chicken and peppers in a shallow glass bowl. Refrigerate at least 30 minutes. Remove chicken and vegetables and set sauce aside. Place half of the chicken in a grill wok and stir-grill over hot coals, basting continuously with sauce until no pink remains. Remove the cooked chicken and add remaining chicken and the peppers to the grill wok and repeat the cooking process. Place all the chicken together in the grill wok along with peppers and baste with sauce and stir-grill for 3 more minutes. Serve immediately. Serves 4 to 6.

POTATOES

Potatoes take a lot of room to grow, so you need plenty of space. One little seed potato can erupt into foliage so massive that it will crowd out anything else in the garden. I plant seed potatoes which I've cut into inch-square chunks. I put them in the soil, about four inches deep, about a foot and a half apart, with the eyes or sprouts facing up. Sweet potatoes, on the other hand, need to be started in containers of moist sand and kept at a constant 80 degrees for the first month and 70 degrees after that, until the rooted sprouts are big enough to set out.

I plant in spring after the ground warms up. My soil is nitrogen rich, so I've got to add phosphorous and potassium if I want any potatoes at all. As the potato vines grow, I add more soil, mounding it up around the plant as it matures. This ensures that the potatoes will be protected from sun and have good moisture for growing. You have to wait until the foliage turns yellow-brown before digging up the spuds. I cut the vines and let the potatoes sit in the ground a few more days to harden the skins. Then I use a spading fork to dig them up.

Real farmers store them for an additional two weeks, in an unlit place with high humidity where the temperature must never go above 60 degrees, nor below 40 degrees. If warmer, the potatoes will sprout; if cooler, the starch turns to sugar. The potatoes must sit in burlap bags and be stacked with care. And it must be dark—for if they are exposed to light, they will turn a greenish color and are not good to eat. Since I don't have a root cellar, my only alternative is to keep my basement dark for potato storage. This forces me to fumble blindly about, washing whites with colors, and making batiks out of Tommy Helfiger shirts. Therefore I dig potatoes and grill them on the spot. I *need* light in my basement. I will not give up white shirts for a pound of potatoes. Never. Maybe for a bushel, but that's pushing it.

Grilled Baby Potatoes
with Olive Oil and Rosemary

4 cups unpeeled new potatoes, washed and scrubbed
3 tablespoons olive oil
1 tablespoon melted butter
2 teaspoons minced fresh rosemary
2 teaspoons minced fresh tarragon
Salt and freshly ground black pepper to taste

Parboil potatoes for two minutes until slightly tender. Combine olive oil, butter, herbs and seasonings. Toss potatoes in mixture until well coated and let sit for 30 minutes to an hour. Remove from mixture with slotted spoon, setting additional liquid aside for basting. Place potatoes on a grill rack brushed with vegetable oil. Grill over medium-high fire turning potatoes often and basting with remaining mixture for about 8 minutes or until the potatoes are tender inside and brown and crispy outside. Serves 3 to 4.

ℒℴ

For those of you who can't wait for the main crop, you can pick baby new potatoes without damaging the plant if you are very careful. Let your fingers do the walking, letting them travel cautiously down beneath the soil searching for tiny tubers. If you don't have enough potatoes for a recipe, buy some more at the store.

Grilled Potatoes with Herbs and Parmesan Cheese

2 medium leeks
5 russet potatoes
2 tablespoons olive oil
1 teaspoon dried rosemary
1 teaspoon dried basil
1 teaspoon dried tarragon
1/4 cup freshly grated Parmesan cheese
Salt and freshly ground pepper

Trim leeks, leaving some green above the white part. Slice in half lengthwise and wash well under running water to remove any dirt. Drain and pat dry and slice into thin strips. Scrub and wash unpeeled potatoes and slice into ovals. Mix together oil and herbs and toss with potatoes and leeks. Place in a grill wok over medium hot coals for 10 to 15 minutes, stirring with wooden paddles, until tender and browned. Remove from fire, add Parmesan cheese and toss again. Season with salt and pepper. Serve immediately. Serves 6 to 8.

Smokey Herbed Potato Salad

6 large Yukon Gold potatoes, unpeeled and washed
1/3 cup vegetable oil, divided
2 teaspoons garlic salt
3 tablespoons tarragon vinegar
1 large leek, finely chopped
1/4 cup chopped fresh chervil
Salt and freshly ground pepper to taste

Coat potatoes with 3 tablespoons oil and sprinkle with garlic salt. Add pre-soaked hickory chips to the grill. Roast potatoes over medium hot coals until done, about 45 minutes. Remove from grill, cool, peel and cut into 1/4 inch slices. Arrange slices in a large shallow bowl and sprinkle with the vinegar. Top with leek and chervil. Drizzle remaining oil over potatoes. Sprinkle with salt and pepper. Cover and let stand at room temperature until ready to serve. Serves 6 to 8.

Smokey Sweet Potatoes

6 sweet potatoes
Olive oil
3 teaspoons garlic salt
Salt, pepper, and honey butter to taste

Wash and scrub potatoes thoroughly. Prick with a fork. Rub with oil and sprinkle with garlic salt. Add some pre-soaked hickory or mesquite chips to the grill and grill sweet potatoes over medium hot coals for about 45 minutes until potatoes are tender when pierced with a fork. To serve, split open and slather with whipped honey butter. Serves 6.

&

You may not give a yam, but American sweet potatoes are pretty tasty and good for you, too. And they have plenty of Vitamin A. To those of you who like to boil them until they are mush and dump marshmallow goo all over them, I have this to say: try a sweet potato roasted whole, and served with whipped honey butter; Thanksgiving will never taste the same.

TOMATOES

If you have no experience sticking plants in the dirt, tomatoes are an excellent choice, because they will produce easily for you. To begin with, go to a nursery in spring and get yourself several varieties of tomato seedlings. Make sure they are leafy, but not too scraggly and leggy, and that the leaves haven't turned brown or yellow. Be sure to ask the nursery folk to provide you with information about the plants, especially with regard to disease resistance, taste, and growing time. Find out what tomato varieties are early producers and what tomatoes need a summer full of sunshine.

There are lots of things to know about tomatoes. For example, determinate tomatoes are bush types that reach about five feet and ripen more quickly than indeterminate tomatoes which are vining types and grow like beanstalks until the first frost. Space your seedlings about four feet apart because, although they may look small and innocent in June, they go absolutely gonzo in July and August, bursting into an uncontrollable eruption of leaf and vine, unless you stake them, trellis them, or surround them with wire plant protectors.

Experienced gardeners usually start tomatoes from seed, purchasing the best and most tasty tomatoes from mail-order companies. If you don't have time or patience to start tomatoes from containers, get some seedlings of the better-known varieties such as Better Boy, Big Boy, Big Girl, or Early Girl which do well for beginners. My personal favorite is Lemon Boy, a yellow, low-acid tomato that tastes terrific, produces a lot of tomatoes, and doesn't give me trouble. I choose beefy tomatoes firm for grilling, along with meaty cherry and pear tomatoes that produce well and taste like someone put all the flavor in the world into them.

Grilled Tomatoes with Blue Cheese and Basil

4 large ripe tomatoes, cut in half (8 pieces)
4 tablespoons crumbled blue cheese
24 fresh basil leaves (3 leaves per each tomato half)

Brush grill rack with oil. Place tomatoes skin side up on the grill over medium high heat and cook for 5 to 8 minutes, until soft. Turn the tomatoes over, place 1/2 tablespoon blue cheese on each, top with basil leaves, and close grill lid. Cook for another minute or two until the cheese is melted. Serves 4 to 6.

Grilled Tomatoes on Focaccia with Aioli

2 large ripe tomatoes, cut in half crosswise
1/3 cup mayonnaise
1 cup olive oil, plus 2 tablespoons for basting
1 tablespoon lemon juice
1 garlic glove, crushed
1/2 teaspoon Worcestershire sauce
2 teaspoons chopped fresh basil
Salt and freshly ground pepper to taste
Focaccia bread

In a small bowl stir together mayonnaise, 1 cup olive oil, garlic, and lemon juice. Add garlic, Worcestershire sauce, basil, and seasonings. Mix thoroughly and chill for up to a day before serving. Brush tomatoes with 2 tablespoons olive oil and place on a greased grill rack over a medium hot fire. Lay tomatoes, cut sides down, on the rack. Cover and grill for three minutes. Turn, cover and grill for another 3 minutes, until heated through. Spread warmed aioli over focaccia bread, place tomatoes on top, and spoon aioli over each tomato half. Serve immediately. Serves 4.

Grilled Oven-Dried Tomatoes

4 pints cherry or plum tomatoes
2 garlic cloves, peeled and sliced (optional)
1 cup olive oil
1/2 cup fresh basil leaves

Slice tomatoes in half, spoon out seeds, and place halves on grill rack flat side down. Bake in oven at 200 degree for 6 to 8 hours, until the tomatoes resemble fruit leather. (If you're using an outdoor gas grill, you can also add pre-soaked wood to the fire for a smokier taste.) In small sterile glass jars, alternate tomatoes, garlic, and basil leaves with oil, until the jar is full. Top with oil, and secure lids, making sure jars are air tight. Place jars in the refrigerator. Makes about 2 pints.

Tomato-Herb Pesto

1 cup fresh tarragon leaves
1/2 cup fresh thyme leaves
1/2 cup fresh oregano leaves
2 large garlic cloves, peeled
1/2 cup freshly grated Parmesan cheese
1/4 cup pine nuts
1 pint *Grilled Oven-Dried Tomatoes*
1/3 cup extra-virgin olive oil
Salt and pepper to taste

Combine the herbs, garlic, cheese, nuts in a food processor along with *Grilled Oven-Dried Tomatoes*. With the machine running, add the olive oil slowly and process to a smooth consistency. Let stand for five minutes. Makes about 2 1/2 cups.

Skewered Lemon-Rosemary Cherry Tomatoes

24 cherry tomatoes
4 sweet onions, peeled and cut into sixths
1/4 cup chopped fresh rosemary leaves (or 2 tablespoons dry)
1/2 cup olive oil
1/4 cup fresh lemon juice
Salt and pepper to taste

Thread cherry tomatoes and onions alternately on pre-soaked wooden skewers. Place skewered vegetables in a large, shallow baking dish. Combine rosemary, olive oil, lemon juice and seasonings and pour over vegetables, coating well. Let marinate for at least 30 minutes, turning two or three times. Remove vegetables, reserving marinade, and lay them on a metal grill rack. Grill over medium-hot fire for about 10-20 minutes, basting frequently until the vegetables are soft. Serves 4.

Quick-Grilled Flank Steak

1 1/2 pounds flank steak

Marinade
1/2 cup olive oil
2 tablespoons lemon juice
1 teaspoon all-purpose seasoning
1/2 teaspoon celery salt
1/2 teaspoon coarsely ground black pepper
1/2 teaspoon onion powder

Combine marinade ingredients and pour over steak in a shallow dish. Marinate in the refrigerator for 4 to 6 hours. Grill steak 4 inches from coals for 15-20 minutes, turning once and basting often with marinade. Before serving, carve into thin slices on diagonal against the grain. Serves 4.

ZUCCHINI AND OTHER SUMMER SQUASH

Anybody can grow squash. It's virtually indestructible as long as you keep it weeded, mulched and protected from cucumber beetles. If you pick the fruits before they reach full maturity, the plant will keep producing and you'll have a huge crop of a delicious vegetable prized by European cooks.

I try to harvest the young squash because they're better-tasting—keeping the length to six inches or less. You can also pick them when they are finger-length. Use a sharp knife to cut them from the vine.

All you need for a small garden is a couple of plants and plenty of room. If you want more than this, you must either (1) have an inexhaustible supply of friends and family who like squash—or (2) plan to travel the world, donating squash wherever you go.

You can plant a hill of summer squash such as crookneck or straightneck squash and intersperse them with zucchini to add more variety. Sow seed when the soil has warmed up and plant about 3 inches deep about 6 feet apart. One of the best types to start with is Burpee Hybrid Zucchini that forms space-saving bushy plants that produce fruit in about a month and a half.

The never-fail zucchini is a garden favorite and comes in many shapes and colors. Green and golden zucchinis are the most popular, and can be sauteed, steamed, fried, pureed, served in salads or grilled to perfection. There's nothing better on a summer day than a bowl of vegetables crowned by grilled summer squash.

Grilled Zucchini and Garden Vegetables

2 small zucchini, sliced
2 small yellow squash, sliced
1 pint cherry tomatoes, whole
1 onion, sliced
1 red bell pepper, sliced
1 green pepper, sliced
1/2 cup Italian salad dressing

Wash and prepare vegetables. Place in a large bowl, add salad dressing, and marinate for 1/2 hour. Pour mixture into a greased grill basket over the sink to drain dressing. Grill for 10 minutes over a hot fire, tossing several times until vegetables are crispy-tender. Serve at once. Serves 6.

Simple Stir-Grilled Summer Squash

4 small summer squash, washed and sliced
1/4 cup olive oil
1 tablespoon each, freshly grated Parmesan, Asiago, and
   Mozzarella cheese
Freshly ground pepper

Lightly toss squash in olive oil. Place in greased grill wok and grill for 10 minutes over a hot fire, tossing several times until squash is crispy-tender. Sprinkle cheeses over squash. Serve with freshly ground pepper to taste. Serves 4.

Herb Grilled Zucchini Squash

4 small zucchini
4 tablespoons olive oil
1/2 cup chopped fresh herbs (chervil, chives, tarragon)
Salt and freshly ground black pepper to taste

Wash, pat dry and slice the squash about an inch thick on the diagonal. Put squash in olive oil in a resealable plastic bag and coat well. Place squash in a greased grill basket and grill over a hot fire for 7 to 10 minutes, tossing every 2 to 3 minutes. The vegetables are done when they're soft, but not mushy. Toss with fresh herbs, salt and pepper. Serves 4.

Stir-Grilled Floribbean-Style Scallops with Vegetables

1 1/2 pounds scallops
12 cherry tomatoes
1 zucchini, sliced
1 yellow squash, sliced

Marinade
2 tablespoons minced shallots
1 tablespoon brown sugar
1 tablespoon prepared mustard
1 tablespoons red wine vinegar
2 tablespoons fresh grapefruit juice
1/2 cup olive oil

In a food processor, mix shallots, brown sugar, mustard, vinegar, grapefruit juice, and seasonings. Add oil in a slow stream until well blended. Set aside. Place scallops and vegetables in a large bowl. Pour marinade over all and marinate for 1 hour in refrigerator. Transfer ingredients to a grill work and drain briefly over sink. Stir-grill in wok over hot coals for 8 to 10 minutes. Serves 4.

Simple,

&

Scrumptious

&

Salads

&

and Sides

Hummus

1 cup canned chickpeas, drained, liquid reserved
1/2 cup tahini
2 garlic cloves, coarsely chopped
1/2 cup fresh lemon juice
1 tablespoon fresh cilantro, minced
Salt and freshly ground pepper to taste
Toasted Oriental Sesame Oil
1/2 teaspoon paprika

Combine chickpeas, tahini, garlic, lemon juice and cilantro in a food processor and puree until smooth, adding chickpea liquid to thin, if needed. Spoon into a small bowl, stir in salt and pepper to taste, and drizzle a little oil on top. Sprinkle with paprika and serve with pita bread or crackers. Makes about 1 1/2 cups.

Onion, Cucumber, and Tomato Raita

1/2 cup onion, chopped
1/2 cup cucumber, seeded and chopped
1 tomato, peeled, seeded and chopped
2 tablespoons fresh cilantro, chopped
1 1/2 teaspoons ground cumin, toasted for 30 seconds in a hot
   skillet
1 cup plain yogurt (not fat free)

Combine all ingredients. Chill for 1 hour before serving. Makes about 2 cups.

Grilled corn, cut off the cob, would make a lovely addition to the Raita.

Garden Caesar Salad

1 large head garden-fresh romaine lettuce
1 large clove garlic, crushed
2 anchovy filets
1/8 teaspoon salt
1/2 teaspoon freshly ground pepper
Juice of 1/2 large lemon
3 tablespoons extra virgin olive oil
1 tablespoon Worcestershire sauce
2 tablespoons egg substitute (such as Eggbeaters or Second
  Nature)
1/2 cup plain croutons

Wash lettuce well. Dry leaves with a towel and chop coarsely. Set aside. Using a fork, mash garlic and anchovies in a large wooden bowl until well blended. Add salt and pepper. Using a wooden spoon, continue mashing mixture until completely spread on the inner bowl surface.

Add lemon juice, olive oil, and Worcestershire sauce. Using the back of the spoon again, spread over inside of bowl for 2 minutes, or until well blended. Add egg substitute and whisk rapidly with a fork until mixture is soupy. Add lettuce and toss until leaves are evenly coated with mixture. Add half of Parmesan cheese and toss. Add croutons and remaining cheese and toss until well mixture. Serve on cold plates. Serves 2 to 4.

Tangy Coleslaw

1 medium head cabbage, shredded
1 to 2 medium onions, diced
3 tablespoons chopped canned pimento, drained
6 tablespoons chopped green bell pepper
3/4 cup white vinegar
1 cup sugar
1/2 teaspoon celery salt
2 teaspoons salt
1 teaspoon celery seed

Combine all ingredients except salt, blend well, and barely cover with boiling water. Let stand for one hour. Pack into jars and refrigerate overnight. Drain and salt to taste before serving. Serves 6.

Hot Slaw

1/4 cup butter
1 medium head cabbage, finely shredded
1/2 cup shredded carrots
1/4 cup cider vinegar
1 tablespoon finely chopped tarragon
1/2 teaspoon pepper

Melt butter in large skillet. Add cabbage, carrots, vinegar, tarragon and pepper. Cover and cook over medium heat for 5 to 7 minutes, stirring frequently. Do not overcook. Serve hot or at room temperature. Serves 6 to 8.

Green Bean Salad

2/3 cup olive oil
1/2 cup white wine vinegar
1/4 teaspoon onion salt
1/4 teaspoon seasoned salt
1/4 teaspoon dry mustard
2 pounds fresh green beans, blanched until crispy-tender

Mix oil, vinegar, and seasonings together. Pour over beans, mixing lightly. Cover and chill overnight. Serves 8.

For a spicy bean salad, add 1/2 teaspoon crushed red pepper flakes and 1 garlic clove, minced finely, to mixture.

Corn Salad with Barbecue Sauce

10 fresh ears of corn, husks removed
1 1/4 cups corn oil
1 1/2 cups barbecue sauce (your favorite), divided
2 red bell peppers, diced in small pieces
2 green bell peppers, diced in small pieces
1 red onion, diced in small pieces
1/4 cup fresh lime juice
2 cloves garlic, finely chopped
1/4 cup Balsamic vinegar
2 bunches fresh cilantro, chopped

Rub corn with 1 cup corn oil. Place on a prepared grill over a hot fire, adding mesquite chips for flavor. While corn is cooking, baste with 1 cup of barbecue sauce. Turn continuously to avoid burning. Remove corn from grill and let cool. In a large bowl combine peppers, onions, lime juice, and garlic. With a sharp knife, remove kernels from each cob of cooled corn. Add corn to pepper mixture, and stir in remaining corn oil, vinegar, chopped cilantro, and remaining 1/2 cup of barbecue sauce. Chill and serve. Serves 16.

I make a lot of this because I like it so much and it keeps so well—several days, tightly covered in the fridge.

Brown Rice and Black Bean Salad

1 1/2 cups brown rice
1 (15 1/2 ounce) can black beans, drained
1 red bell pepper, diced
2 green onions, chopped
2 tablespoons fresh parsley, chopped
Sesame Orange Sauce (from page 18)

Cook rice according to package directions, drain and cool. Add beans, pepper, onions, and parsley; mix well. Add *Sesame Orange Sauce*, mix, cover and refrigerate for at least one hour before serving. Serves 4.

Cilantro-Orange Rice

1 cup water
1 cup fresh squeezed orange juice
2 teaspoons freshly chopped cilantro
1/4 teaspoon salt
1 cup white Basmati, or Texmati rice (or long grain rice)
1 small leek, thinly sliced

Combine water, juice, and salt in a medium saucepan. Bring to a boil and add rice. Let come to a boil, reduce heat, cover and simmer for 15 to 20 minutes or until rice is plump and tender. Remove from heat, stir in leek and cilantro. Cover and let stand five minutes more. Serves 4.

Tabouli Tomato Toss

1 cup fine bulgur
1 1/2 cups boiling water
2 green onions, chopped
4 tablespoons finely chopped fresh mint
4 tablespoons finely chopped fresh parsley
1 carrot, grated
1/2 cup chopped cucumber
2 cups feta cheese
3 large tomatoes, seeded and finely chopped

Dressing
2/3 cup olive oil
1/2 cup fresh lemon juice
2 teaspoons minced garlic
Salt and freshly ground pepper to taste

Combine bulgur and water in large bowl. Cover and let stand for 20 to 25 minutes, until bulgur is tender; drain. Combine dressing ingredients in a small jar with lid and shake to blend. Add dressing to bulgur, mixing well. Add onions, mint, parsley, carrot, cucumber and cheese and mix together. Cover tightly and refrigerate for at least two hours before serving. About 30 minutes before serving, add tomatoes to mixture and toss together. Correct seasonings. Serves 6.

Pasta with Cherry Tomatoes

1 pound cooked pasta
1 1/2 pounds cherry tomatoes, halved
2 garlic cloves minced
2 shallots, minced
1/4 cup extra virgin olive oil
3/4 cup loosely packed fresh basil leaves
Salt and freshly ground pepper to taste

In a large pan sauté tomatoes together with garlic, shallots, olive oil, salt and pepper. Simmer over moderate heat until the tomato juices have blended into the mixture. Remove from heat while the tomatoes still have their shape. Chop basil and add it to the sauce, mixing well. Add additional seasoning to taste. Place drained pasta into a large bowl, add the sauce, and toss well. Serve immediately. Serves 8 to 10 as a side dish.

Creamy Risotto

1 small onion, minced
1/2 cup butter, divided
1 1/2 cups uncooked Arborio rice
1 teaspoon saffron threads
4 cups chicken stock
2 tablespoons freshly grated Parmesan cheese

Sauté onion in 1/4 cup butter until lightly browned. Add rice and mix well. Soften saffron in 2 tablespoons of chicken stock. Add remaining stock to rice and bring to a boil. Simmer, covered, over low heat for 25 minutes, stirring frequently. Add remaining 1/4 cup butter and saffron. Simmer, uncovered, over low heat for 5 minutes more. Spoon onto a serving dish and sprinkle with Parmesan cheese. Serves 6.

Couscous with Moroccan-Style Garden Vegetables

2 cups chicken stock
1 1/2 cup couscous
2 chopped green onions
1 yellow bell pepper, seeded and chopped
1 cucumber, seeded and chopped
1 tomato, stemmed and chopped
2 tablespoons fresh snipped chives
Salt and pepper to taste
Moroccan Dressing

Bring chicken stock to a boil and pour over couscous in a large bowl. Let stand to absorb liquid, about 5 minutes, then fluff with a fork. Toss vegetables together with *Moroccan Dressing* and serve over couscous. Serves 4.

Moroccan Dressing
1 cup olive oil
1/3 cup lemon juice
1/4 cup chopped fresh parsley
2 garlic cloves, crushed
1 teaspoon ground cumin
Salt and freshly ground pepper to taste

Mix together oil, lemon juice, parsley, garlic, cumin, and seasonings. Makes about 1 1/4 cups.

The Moroccan Dressing *is also delicious when used as a marinade for grilled chicken.*

Polenta

4 1/2 cups water
1/2 teaspoon salt
1 cup polenta
2 tablespoons butter

Boil water with salt. Add polenta slowly, stirring constantly to avoid lumps. Reduce heat and cook for 25 to 30 minutes. Mixture will pull away from sides of pan when done. Place in a 10-inch pie pan, and let cool at room temperature until firm. Serves 4.

Polenta is a wonderfully versatile side dish. Serve it warm or cold, plain or topped with your favorite tomato sauce, pesto, or with grilled peppers and onions. For a very special treat, slice into wedges, brush lightly with olive oil and grill for about 8 to 10 minutes per side.

RECIPE INDEX

Grains and Pastas

Brown Rice and Black Bean Salad, 81
Buckwheat Noodles in Sesame-Orange Sauce, 18
Cilantro-Orange Rice, 81
Couscous with Moroccan-Style Garden Vegetables, 84
Creamy Risotto, 83
Pasta with Cherry Tomatoes, 83
Penne Pasta in Tomato and Basil Sauce with Grilled Greens, 50
Polenta, 85
Tabouli Tomato Toss, 82

Meats

Garlic Marinated Strip Steaks, 23
Grilled Pork Tenderloin Kebobs—Southern Comfort Style, 29
Grilled Herbed Hamburgers, 35
Grilled Ham Slice with Brown Sugar and Butter, 51
Mesquite-Flavored Pork Patties with Grilled Leeks, 53
Quick-Grilled Flank Steak, 71
Scallion Stuffed Italian Sausage, 56

Poultry

Grilled Chicken Wings, 43
Grilled Duck Breast with Red Pepper Butter, 62
Herb-and-Honey Grilled Chicken Breasts, 47
Minted Casablanca Chicken Strips, 31
Stir-Grilled Chicken with Tangerine and Ginger Sauce, 63

Salads

Vegetables

Mushroom, Portobello Mozzarella "Burgers," 35
Onions, Red Grilled Sliced, 55
Onions, Grilled Garden, 56
Onions, Grilled with Tomatoes in Basil Vinaigrette, 57
Peppers, Hot and Spicy Grilled, 61
Pepper Medley, Grilled, 62
Potatoes, Grilled Baby with Olive Oil & Rosemary, 65
Potatoes, Grilled with Herbs & Parmesan Cheese, 66
Potato, Smokey Herbed Salad, 66
Radicchio, Grilled with Garlic-Braised Mushrooms, 51
Shallots, Grilled with Tarragon Butter, 42
Snow Peas, Italian-Style with Peppers, 59
Sweet Potatoes, Smokey, 67
Squash, Simple Stir-Grilled Summer, 73
Tomatoes, Grilled with Blue Cheese and Basil, 69
Tomatoes, Grilled on Focaccia with Aioli, 69
Tomatoes, Grilled Oven-Dried, 70
Tomatoes, Skewered Lemon-Rosemary Cherry, 71
Vegetables, Stir-Grilled with Island Marinade, 28
Zucchini, Grilled with Garden Vegetables, 73
Zucchini, Herb Grilled, 74

ABOUT THE AUTHOR

Author, journalist, and speaker, Shifra Stein, enjoys growing food almost as much as she likes eating it. The former restaurant critic for *The Kansas City Star* newspaper, claims she can eat her weight in tomatoes and green beans any day. Her travel guides and cookbooks extol the merits of a simpler, less hectic lifestyle, where it makes sense to slow down long enough to smell the lemon verbena.

Ms. Stein began gardening several years ago. What was supposed to have been a brief respite from a hectic lifestyle, has become a way of life for the globe-trotting journalist who has penned over 20 food and travel guides and hundreds of articles for newspapers and magazines.

Ms. Stein is the creator of the acclaimed Day Trips™ series for Globe Pequot Press for the cities of Kansas City, Nashville, San Antonio-Austin, Phoenix-Tucson-Flagstaff, Baltimore, Cincinnati, and Houston. In addition she has authored several cookbooks which include *Kansas City Cuisine,* with Karen Adler, and *All About Bar-B-Q Kansas City-Style,* with Rich Davis. Her other books include *Heart of America: Kansas City,* and *Unlocking the Power Within: Journaling For Personal and Professional Growth.*

Ms. Stein offers workshops, presentations, and personal and professional enrichment seminars based on her books. She is available for interviews and speaking engagements. For information call the publisher, Pig Out Publications, at (816) 531-3119.